"Brenda is a cancer survivor, a talented broadcast journalist, but most importantly, a strong woman of faith with a servant's heart. Let her encourage you in this book, and let God's healing begin in your life."

— JAMES SPANN, CBM
ABC 33/40, Chief Meteorologist

"A gifted communicator, Brenda combines thorough biblical teaching with an ability to apply the comfort of Scripture to life's most painful and challenging circumstances."

— DON HAWKINS, DMin, president, Southeastern Bible College

Other New Hope books
by Brenda Ladun

*Getting Better, Not Bitter: A Spiritual
Prescription for Breast Cancer*

*Behind the Scenes of Breast Cancer: A News Anchor
Tells Her Story of Body and Soul Recovery*
(Includes DVD)

Encouraged

Encouraged

An INSPIRING JOURNEY WITH REAL-LIFE STORIES of HOPE

Brenda Ladun
Award-Winning ABC News Anchor

NEW HOPE
P U B L I S H E R S
Gospel-Centered. Missions-Driven.

BIRMINGHAM, ALABAMA

New Hope® Publishers
P. O. Box 12065
Birmingham, AL 35202-2065
NewHopeDigital.com
New Hope Publishers is a division of WMU®.

Library of Congress Control Number: 2013952368

Cover Design: Kay Bishop
Interior Design: Glynese Northam

ISBN-10: 1-59669-394-0
ISBN-13: 978-1-59669-394-4
N144103• 0114 • 3M1

Table of Contents

11   Introduction

17   Chapter 1:   WHY STORMS?

29   Chapter 2:   STORMS GOD ALLOWS

43   Chapter 3:   STORMS OF "BUSYNESS"

53   Chapter 4:   STORMS FROM SIN

71   Chapter 5:   FACING STORMS WITH PRAYER

89   Chapter 6:   STAYING STRONG IN THE STORM

111 Chapter 7:   FELLOWSHIP IN THE STORM

127 Chapter 8:   WHEN YOU THINK YOU
                  CAN'T GO ON

137 Chapter 9:   RACING INTO HIS ARMS

149 Chapter 10: THE GLORY OF TRUSTING IN GOD

165 Chapter 11: ENCOURAGED

177 Chapter 12: CALLED TO ENCOURAGE

Dedication

I dedicate this book to my mother. When I think of her, I am reminded of the encouragement she has given to me throughout my life. No matter what I bring to her, she *finds* encouraging words. She is a wonderful example of God's unconditional love and of someone who follows His instructions.

Thank you, Mom, for teaching me how to get through tough times. You showed me how to continue to trust the Lord through each heartbreak, challenge, and uphill battle in my life. Mom, thank you for teaching me how to pray and praise and thank the Lord for all of my blessings.

Introduction

In writing this book, I spent time processing some of the chaos in my own life that can often feel like a storm of sorts. I often felt I had more to do than I had hours in the day. I drove my kids to practices and made sure everyone was fed. Then I threw a load of laundry into the washer and sat down to steal a few moments for writing. I asked the Lord what He wanted me to say in this book. Somehow amidst the busyness, He helped me carve out time to focus on Him and write the things I am now sharing with you.

This is not the first book that I've written to process life's chaos. In *Getting Better, Not Bitter*, and *Behind the Scenes of Breast Cancer*, I invited you inside my journey. Although I share here some personal stories touched on in my first book about the first leg of my journey through cancer, this book will be different, as God has continued to teach me about His character—and mine—through my *second* leg of my cancer marathon, which began as I completed my second book. How He has counterattacked my chaos is nothing short of miraculous. The results of focusing on and trusting in Him for my personal life and professional work are continual stories of encouragement that I not only reflect on but also share for His glory.

While I was writing, promotions for this book began, and "winds" whipped up enthusiasm for *Encouraged*. New Hope asked me to add a substantial number of additional stories and to tape more segments for the accompanying DVD! One piece of chaos included a house under construction. Our refrigerator leaked, and we needed to replace most of the flooring on the first level of our home. On many a morning, we woke up to a number of crews—demolition, construction, clean-up, move-out, and floor—working on our house.

But through the chaos, the Lord—Jesus, my Rock—continued to show me that with Him all things are possible. I do not pretend nor profess to have all the answers to provide relief from life's storms. However, I know where those answers can be found. I pray when the waters get choppy, as well as when they're calm. I look to God's Word and His plans. I know I can call out to the Lord every day, and I am grateful He loves me enough to listen. And He always answers!

The Lord has placed *you* on my heart. I know you have faced challenges—maybe heartbreaking ones. Perhaps you lost a loved one. Maybe the person you looked up to and loved the most hurt you deeply. Perhaps it was a spouse, parent, child, sibling, or friend. Maybe your own body let you down with an illness. Or maybe you experienced disappointment at school or on your job. Possibly, you have been abandoned, or abused physically, verbally, or emotionally.

I want to tell you I am so very sorry for the things that hurt you in your life. Although I can't erase your hurts, no matter how much I would desire to, I can encourage you that God grows us and strengthens us through the tough times and challenges of life — even through the brokenness, pain, and waiting.

> *"Praise be to the God and Father of our Lord Jesus Christ, the Father of compassion and the God of all comfort, who comforts us in all our troubles, so that we can comfort those in any trouble- with the comfort we ourselves receive from God"* (2 Corinthians 1:3–4).

I am so convinced of this truth that I want to share intimate details about the struggles and victories in my own life, as well as inspiring stories from many others, to help you see that God is our Help in the storms. May you allow the Lord's transforming love and grace to change your life . . . and allow God to lead you! I pray these words will help you understand the powerful transformation that can happen in your life if you let go and let God. My prayer is that you will allow God into your heart so He can be your haven and your healer. So you can be cleansed by His blood!

Ultimately, we have confidence in the knowledge that He has a *better* plan — for this life and the one to come. Our lives down here and in eternity are gifts from the Lord. May this book help you find an *eternal* purpose in whatever storm you may be facing. Then may you put your faith into action by becoming Jesus' hands and feet. Be encouraged, and then help encourage others.

Our Key Scripture

"*I have told you these things, so that in me you may have peace. In this world you will have trouble. But take heart! I have overcome the world*" (JOHN 16:33).

Why Storms?

COVERING THE NEWS

As a newswoman, I have learned that, as the day unfolds, someone's life will change suddenly and forever. Someone will face a tragedy or will experience great joy. Whether caused by an accident, an act of violence, or a kind deed, change can come in an instant—for better or for worse.

It could be a mining accident, a shooting, drowning, fire, or car crash. But the news will also air stories of hope and perseverance. On any particular day there might be stories of joy . . . babies being born, engagements, ground breakings—hope for the future. Some people's lives will change because of their choices; others will be changed because of someone else's. I guess you can call it *life*!

I have also learned that no matter whether the news is bad or good—even if there's no news at all—the Lord is walking with me every step of the way. I am not alone. Whether it's a good or bad day, focusing on Christ keeps me on solid ground.

When I am caught up in other things, or even in myself and my own troubles, I become frustrated and empty. Sometimes pride, anxiety, fear, frustration, pain, impatience, and the storms of life push and shove to try to challenge Christ's lordship in my life. However, when I put my focus back on Christ and trust Him to produce good fruit in any situation, my faith is strengthened and He is glorified.

A typical day of mine once began with fixing a doorknob. The front door would always stick, and the lock never wanted to cooperate either. So it was out with the old and broken and in with the new. Funny, because my day ended with my also having to fix a broken zipper on my pants.

In between those two fixes, I covered a plane crash in Birmingham. Pieces of the plane were sprinkled on the ground where children once played baseball. Two pilots flying the cargo plane died in the crash. There was no fixing this devastation, nor the hearts that would be broken.

How can you have peace in the midst of great loss? How can you have peace during and after a storm? How can you have peace in everyday chaos? How can you get through what seems like an impossible dilemma? "Cast your cares on the Lord and he will sustain you; he will never let the righteous be shaken" (Psalm 55:22).

ON THE HOME FRONT

To give you a personal example, back in the late 1920s my grandfather once stayed up all night to read the Bible to a dying friend. Back then, no one really knew what a virus was; the local doctor just knew that something was robbing this man's life. But later they discovered typhoid in the man's drinking water. My grandfather drank the water all during the night, and he too died a short time later. Overnight this turned my grandmother into a single mom who had to feed, care for, and keep a roof over the heads of four boys during the Depression. She even took in boarders to help make ends meet. My grandmother, whom we lovingly called Baba, had to rely on the Lord to help her in her time of need.

I remember asking my sister what she remembered most about Baba. She said it was that my grandmother had prayed constantly. No doubt becoming a single mom when her youngest son was only six years old drove her to pray and completely trust in God to carry her through.

And the Lord did provide for her during this storm. She remarried the man that I grew up knowing as my grandfather, or as we called him, Gigi. Baba had received help in raising her four boys, and they all grew up to be fine men.

So you are in a storm; whatcha gonna do? Hide in a closet? Or will you face the storm with God at your side, guiding you through it, comforting you and molding you into the person He created you to be?

More than once during my breast cancer battle and afterward, I felt like I was being refined. I was roasted, toasted, and radiated. Not long after the death of my father, heavy rains caused the creek in our backyard to rise almost to its banks. A huge tree in the soggy soil fell and damaged the bridge that spanned the rushing torrent. When bad things happen in our family, they come in droves.

Maybe there is something in your life that you didn't plan on. Maybe you wished for, prayed for, and counted on that "happily ever after," but it didn't turn out that way. Cancer, death, finances, relational problems. Everyone gets something sooner or later. We can choose to let the bad thing define us or we can reach up for God's healing. We can resist His refining storms, or be open to how this tough situation can mold us for the good of His kingdom.

Every now and then I have to tell myself, "Wake up and smell the coffee, Cinderella." Those fairy tales where Prince Charming saves the beautiful damsel are—in fact—fairy tales. Getting the prince to marry you, sweeping you off into the sunset, is really just the beginning of the challenges, trials, and tribulations. If you really want to prepare kids for life, tell them stories of real-life warriors. Who are your Christian heroes—or even those from your own heritage? I have mine and I'm sure you have yours.

PRUNES AND MINTS

Speaking of kids, one Sunday morning almost a year after my surgery, the Bible lesson was about how God prunes away what is useless. I had been pruned in many ways during the last year. The Gospel of John says it this way:

> "I am the true vine, and my Father is the gardener. He cuts off every branch in me that bears no fruit, while every branch that does bear fruit he prunes so that it will be even more fruitful. . . . No branch can bear fruit by itself; it must remain in the vine. Neither can

you bear fruit unless you remain in me. I am the vine;
you are the branches. If you remain in me and I in
you, you will bear much fruit; apart from me you can
do nothing" (15:1–2,4–5).

That Sunday morning in class, we were having a good discussion about that Scripture. I wanted to shout, "I've been pruned!" But just as I got ready to share my thoughts, class was dismissed. So I'll share with you now how I've been pruned.

Before I had cancer, things like hair, makeup, furniture, new clothes, and sending my kids to the right summer camps were extremely important to me. But now those take a backseat to the truly important things in life—things like spending time with my friends and family, talking with someone who's just been diagnosed with cancer, or taking care of myself by resting or running.

I realize there's a wealth of information in the Bible. I like to discover verses that apply to my life. I take time to appreciate the incredible world the Lord made. Fussing over the little things in life like traffic jams or a burnt dinner just doesn't seem worth it anymore. I look for the good and embrace it. There is so much good in our world.

Now, my favorite thing is to listen to my children. Things like, "Mommy, if this is a free country, why isn't everything free. Why do we have to pay for groceries?"

Or this one made me chuckle: "Mommy, how did you get those colored marshmallows hard and to taste like mint?"

"Honey, those *are* mints, not marshmallows," I answered.

PEACE IN THE STORM

When I speak to groups about these good things that have been born out of my cancer battles, I often like to ask the question: "Who does not have a problem?" Then people look around, and I point out that we are all brothers and sisters and we all have problems. Some may be big, some may be small, but we all share the fact that we have to deal with something.

Very rarely does anyone ever raise a hand. If people do, then they have realized how to let go of problems and let God handle them. The Lord has humbled me time and time again. After some of the struggles we had at my house with health and much more, I have learned to trust Him with all my heart in the darkest of times.

The fact is, in this life we will all have challenges. But if we don't focus on God, we can find those challenges pulling us into a pit. You may be in relationships with people who cause you to be anxious or on edge. It just seems like no matter what you do, you can't please them. Or perhaps you worry about your children, their grades, their welfare, their future. Maybe you worry about money, supporting your family, or something else.

Just watching the news can cause anxiety. With talk of terrorist attacks, murders, and financial woes, it's easy to understand that we live in a stressful world. There are even television shows about people who spend thousands of dollars to build bunkers in their homes in case of a catastrophic event. We are constantly warned by federal health officials to get this or that vaccine to fend off the next big bug.

Then there's the pressure to perform in a competitive world. Performing up to par isn't easy. According to the world, we are supposed to be supermoms, superwives, have the brightest smiles and the freshest smelling laundry! Watching just a few minutes of television can convince me to make a mad dash to the closest drugstore to snatch up some of that cream that will make me look 20 years younger!

The list can be long: health, family, job, finances, the world, death? Being alone? Are you focusing on the problems and not the solution? God can be the solution to any worry in your life. God has an answer for it all. He promises us we are not alone. We can turn over all our cares and worries to Him.

But that surrender is hard to achieve. We recently featured a tornado survivor on the news. He is 89 years old. He lost everything in the storm! You may be stunned to find out he is the happiest man I have ever encountered. He was helping others pick up the pieces after the storm and encouraging them with a positive word.

He said, "Like I told my late wife, God rest her sweet soul, what does worrying accomplish? What problem does it ever solve?"

He knows the true power is in trusting God to take care of his worries. That is so hard to do . . . but you can do it! This book is designed to encourage you to get through life . . . good days and bad. Proverbs 12:25 (NLT) says, "Worry weighs a person down; an encouraging word cheers a person up."

There have been times I'm ashamed to say that I started my day swinging with my own strength. I tried to tackle the world, get all the tasks done, solve the world's problems, and put dinner in the Crock-Pot. As I look back, I see that many of those days were uphill battles because I did not put the Lord first. I did not consult His Word. I did not pray, "Lord, unfold my day for me. Show me my steps. Show me Your will in this day."

But on the days I consult with Him and pray that prayer . . . watch out! Magnificent things happen. One of the greatest blessings I praise God for is the fact that I can find peace in a storm-filled life. Even when my laundry is up around my ears, or when life is crashing down around me, I can be content with the Lord's hand guiding me. Trust Him in the midst of your storms, and He'll give you His peace too.

Our Key Scripture

"And we know that in all things God works for the good of those who love him, who have been called according to his purpose" (ROMANS 8:28).

CHAPTER 2

Storms God Allows

*E*ach time I had cancer I had to use a specific type of chemo. Each treatment had specific side effects. The first time the chemo sapped my strength, gave me a gastronomical nightmare, and caused my hair to fall out. The second time I had *Taxotere*. It raked my hands and feet with painful, burning, pins and needles, followed by numbness. The very treatments that are supposed to clear the cancer can also threaten your life. But I had to believe that even the worst parts of these storms were ordained by my loving heavenly Father for some good purpose that I couldn't yet see.

DEPRESSION AND DIVORCE

Joie Black also learned of the eventual goodness of God's plans in the storms she faced. She had dreamed of that fairy-tale ending that so many of us wish for. Like I said earlier, we all want our Prince Charming to carry us off into the sunset and away from our problems. Then we can have our families and it's happily ever after, right? Ha! Wrong! That's when the truly hard struggles begin.

Loving our husbands and children so much also comes with hurts. Your heart hurts when they hurt. Your heart hurts when someone is cruel to them. You hurt because you find out, as we all do, that our Prince Charmings are not perfect. None of us are. The only perfect One who came to this earth was Jesus. And we soon find out, after we get off Prince Charming's white horse to start our lives, that problems are an integral part of life. As Joie says, life is messy, and life can hurt, but the Lord is our Rock.

Joie got married to the love of her life. It all seemed like a dream come true. But as they progressed through married life and tried to have a baby, they soon found out they could not have children. So, after praying about it, they decided to adopt. After a long process, she and her husband were blessed when they adopted a daughter.

Joie's husband, Andy Black, began struggling with depression. Every doctor they went to tried, but could not help. This went on for almost 20 years. The depression at times prevented him from functioning. Sometimes he did not even want to get out of bed. He also struggled with fear and panic attacks. He was an extrovert, which was unusual for a man with depression. But it enabled him to share his struggle with others and ask for help. Nothing worked. Chemical imbalances, enablers, pressures of keeping up, fear of failure, the Enemy. . . . Joie believes that all these factors pushed her husband to the point where he took own life. "We had tried everything. . . . He had reached out for help. . . . But he had finally hit bottom and took his own life. It was a painful, hard road. . . ."

There was confusion, but Joie clung to God all the more. Even though the storm hurt, the Lord used it to develop her.

He also used the people around her. She says that on the day her husband died, she sensed God's presence and peace. People started showing up at her house. She said it was like she was in a play where all the actors knew their parts but her. She was the main character, but she had no idea what to do. She says the Lord started carrying her, and He showed her what needed to be done.

She asked God if Satan had won. But the Lord told her that her husband was with Him in heaven. She feels that Satan won a battle but not the war. Satan cannot separate us from God. She believes what the Lord told her. She knows her husband was a Christian and that he is in heaven now.

Joie has seen Romans 8:28 work right in front of her. The Lord uses her husband's story for good to help others who come to her and share their struggles with mental illness. She helps many others that are suffering in silence, because they don't know what to do with depression.

She has learned the three Ds: *discipline, development,* and *deployment.* Discipline to obey God's Word, development to grow as a Christian, and deployment to carry out God's commands. Joie says depression is an illness so many people suffer with in silence, because it's an illness people don't want to talk about. Life can be messy for Christians—for everyone.

When you deal with mental illness, there is no elixir to heal it. Not with medicine or counseling. But Joie says she still has hope, and that hope is in a redemptive God who uses our smaller stories in His bigger story.

"My messy story is just a part of a bigger, better story, and one day I will know the rest of the story and that my life's struggles expand God's purpose. We have hope for a future in heaven. That's the real hope. When Jesus came, He started redeeming and restoring. It's like I have a blindfold on sometimes. He only lets me peek at the future. Faith is in His promises. I don't think there are guarantees for this life as much as we want. I have a Rock, even though each day is rough.

Joie *does* hurt. It *is* hard. She says, "You can hold joy and hurt at the same time. Andy didn't pretend things were happy; he did cry. It's OK to hurt. The Lord is with you in the pain. He doesn't take an eraser to wipe it away. You often hear, 'Trust in God. It'll help you feel better.' The sting is gone, but the pain of grief is still there. With God's help, I am in a better place. I grieve for my daughter, what she is missing. He is walking her through it. I remain confident of this: I will see the goodness of the Lord in the land of the living."

Her words remind me of some wonderful Scriptures. "Wait for the Lord; be strong and take heart and wait for the Lord" (Psalm 27:14). "For the Lord God is a sun and shield; the Lord bestows favor and honor; no good thing does he withhold from those whose walk is blameless. Lord Almighty, blessed is the one who trusts in you" (Psalm 84:11–12).

Joie's not the only one looking for encouragement in her storms. My friend Gwen had a bike accident and almost lost her life. During the ambulance ride to the hospital, she found out that she had a broken pelvis, broken leg, and more injuries. She was a single mom as a result of a bad marriage, and she remembers panicking about who would take care of her son, her horses, and her dogs. But then she said that she found Christ in the ambulance! She said it was weird. She had started to pray, "Oh God, help!" and then this comforting emotion washed over her. She felt like God was saying, "Trust me. I have your back, Gwen."

When I heard the news of her accident, I rushed to the hospital, prepared for the worst. They had told me at the TV station that she was badly banged up. But when I walked into the room, my pretty friend was hurt and lying in the bed, but she could talk. You will never guess what she said.

"I know this looks bad, but this isn't the worst thing that's ever happened to me. That man I married is the worst thing that ever happened to me. This is nothing compared to that." I smiled, glad that God had seemed to get a hold of her and let her know He was in control. He loved her, and He was going to get her through this.

Gwen had no worries after that. Every bill she had worried about was paid for. Friends rose up and met every need she and her son had. She said God showed her He would help her through anything. Trust!

During her loss and realizing all she could lose, she found Christ right beside her, and she saw His love demonstrated through others who surrounded her. She found joy in understanding how much God loved her and would meet her needs if she just trusted Him.

MODERN-DAY JOB

Every time I hear of stories like Joie's and Gwen's, I think of Job. He lost everything: children, servants, livestock, and buildings.

But throughout his storms, he remains faithful to God. He still admits he's hurting; he calls it unrelenting pain. But he is encouraged in that pain through the fact that he is able to stay true to God through it all. He does not deny God. He loves Him, honors Him, and still worships Him.

Job is one of the most powerful stories of loss and getting through tough times. How would any of us react? Could you have still praised God after such incredible loss and pain? Job's own wife couldn't understand it, and they definitely disagreed on this point. "His wife said to him, 'Are you still maintaining your integrity? Curse God and die!'" (Job 2:9).

Job was committed to God. He didn't look to Him for only what He could give him, he looked to God as his Everything, as his Father in heaven. Job was patient and waited on the Lord, and the Lord replenished his life and family and belongings. Like Job, another man I met a man also lost everything. And he, too, experienced God's mercy.

I was making the bed. I had just gotten the kids off to school. My phone rang.

"Hello, Brenda. This is Sonya Smith. Have I got a story for you!"

It was a few weeks until Christmas. Sonya and her friend and animal rescue volunteer Evelyn Neeley decided they wanted to help someone for Christmas. Evelyn said she knew the perfect person to help, but she had no idea how to get a hold of him.

During the previous summer, Evelyn had spotted a man named Chris walking his dog Max along a street in Bessemer, Alabama. It was a hundred degrees that day. Evelyn had asked the young man if he and his dog needed water. The young man said no and pulled a dog dish and a container of water out of his backpack. He explained to Evelyn that he lived nearby. During their conversation, she asked him more about where he lived. He finally admitted he was living in a tent.

When she offered to help him, he refused. He was too proud to accept help. He had been a loner, ever since a drunk driver took the lives of his wife and baby boy. Evelyn didn't want to leave the dog-and-man duo alone to fend for themselves, but she knew there was nothing she could do to change his mind. So she gave him her phone number and told him to call her if he ever needed something. That was July.

Five months later, Evelyn and Sonya remembered the young man and his dog, but they had no idea how to get in touch with him. Here's how God works. The very next day, Chris called Evelyn for help.

Evelyn says she knew that God had intervened. As Sonya and Evelyn were praying for someone to help, Chris had hit bottom. It was rainy and cold. Water was running through his tent. He looked at his dog. Max had his head hung low, and Chris knew he had to do something—if not for himself, then for his dog. Chris cried out to God and said, "OK, God. I need some help." Chris figured it was time, and Max deserved better, so he called the kind woman named Evelyn.

That's when things started to turn around for him. Sure God rescued him physically, by providing a roof over his head. He provided food for him, too, through those sweet ladies. And they found him a car and a job. But even more importantly, He rescued Chris spiritually. That was God's work.

Can you see what happened here? Chris called out for God's help when he hit rock bottom. It took the misery of the storm for him and his dog to be in such discomfort that he cried out to God for help. "But when we cried out to the Lord, he heard our cry and sent an angel and brought us out of Egypt" (Numbers 20:16).

The most touching thing Chris said was that he started to care about himself because others showed they cared for him. Yes, the Lord answers our cries. He operates to mold us in love, and that love can be life changing.

I recently saw a movie that is patterned after a real-life young man whose story is similar to Chris's. He was in college when he found out his mother had died of a drug overdose. It hit him so hard that he quit school and became a prodigal son. He was mad at God. He tried to hide from the pain by turning to alcohol.

But God sent a friend who was also hurting from his own storm: he had divorced at a young age. Together they rediscovered their faith, and the love of God helped them heal. The two men produced a movie called *The Prodigal*. It is a modern-day version of the Bible story. He learned to turn his focus from his pain toward Christ. "I can do all things through Christ who strengthens me!" (Philippians 4:13 KJV).

Whether in the movies or in real life, God can use our hurts and tough times to mold us. Especially in today's world, we need something to hold on to.

"Have no fear of sudden disaster or of the ruin that overtakes the wicked, for the Lord will be at your side and will keep your foot from being snared" (Proverbs 3:25).

Internationally, just look at the disaster in Japan. First the earthquake, then the tsunami, and then the nuclear disasters. And the hits just keep on coming with the aftershocks! Nationally, tornados ravage our cities every year. It takes years to restore things for those who lost everything.

Personally, although it might seem trivial, I lost my hair— twice—thanks to chemo. When I was first diagnosed with the C word, I was tempted to cover all the mirrors around the house. I know about the comb-over. But at some point, as my hair continued to thin, I had to face it. I couldn't hide it, nor could I deny there was a change up on top.

The reason this has so much meaning for me is that I have found myself doing the comb-over with other things in life. Pretending everything is OK when it's not. How many people do the comb-over on Sunday mornings? Put the smile on and hope for the best? Is there anyone here that does not have a problem? Now that would be a news story. The fact is, we are all sisters. We all face something painful.

We can be honest with God about the hurts in our lives; we don't have to try to do the comb-over for things that have hurt us. Face it, deal with it, forgive, and move on. And whatever it is you are trying to comb over, seek the Lord's will first, and He will make your path straight. "But seek first his kingdom and his righteousness, and all these things will be given to you as well" (Matthew 6:33).

Yes, God sometimes allows us to walk through tough times, but only to lead us to our blessings. Going through tough times helps our faith grow. Think about events in your own life. Didn't you grow more during the tough times? Through the crises in my life, I learned I could call out to Him, and He would hear my prayers and answer. I grew more spiritually during those times than during the good times. Through cancer, I learned to trust God, and I truly learned how much He loves me.

 Surrender your crisis and hurts to the Lord in prayer with thanksgiving.

Our Key Scriptures

"*Am I now trying to win the approval of human beings, or of God? Or am I trying to please people? If I were still trying to please people, I would not be a servant of Christ*" (GALATIANS 1:10).

"*The* LORD *answered, 'You are worried and upset about many things, but only one thing is needed'*" (LUKE 10:41–42).

Storms of "Busyness"

A TYPICAL MOM?

My mother has chuckled about the fact that, other than *Mama* and *Dada*, my first word was *busy*. I'd watch my Mom flutter around the house cleaning, and she'd say "busy, busy, busy," and I'd repeat the same. I never really walked; I crawled, then I ran. She thinks it's funny that I've been busy ever since.

Why can't I be one of those sit-by-the-sea-and-ponder people? I guess because God has a plan for each one of us. For me, He must have said, "This one will be busy."

Moms know. From the time mom gets up in the morning until the time she drops into bed after cleaning up and giving goodnight kisses, our days are packed full. And many women balance a career with their responsibilities at home and extended family, as I do.

As a television news anchor, I've spent my days at work developing and producing stories for multiple newscasts. No two days are exactly the same in this job. Chaos can take over at any time because of breaking news. We have to be ready to respond at a moment's notice to deliver the story. For instance, when a truck carrying dangerous chemicals crashes on an interstate, we warn drivers to steer clear of the dangerous area. It's a job where the information we deliver can make a difference in many lives, thankfully.

What's a typical day like in the life of a news anchor? My workday can start when most other people's days wind down. Work can begin with a strategy meeting. Anchors, reporters, producers, photographers, and the news director meet to talk about the important stories of the day. The producer decides which items will be in the newscast. During the afternoon, I might shoot or write a story that will air that evening.

While I enjoy anchoring, reporting in the community makes for even more fun. I think staying connected is important. I like talking to people. Helping resolve an elderly woman's phone bill problem or talking to a 76-year-old marathon runner is a kick for me.

I have an awesome family life and professional job, but sometimes I get too busy to enjoy the gifts.

Cancer helped open my eyes to the fact that every day is a gift from God, one that we can open and enjoy just as we would a Christmas present. Before cancer, I didn't see the big picture; I only saw the busy work, much like Martha of Bethany. The Bible describes how Jesus came to Martha's home (Luke 10:38–42). Her sister, Mary, sat at Jesus' feet listening to Him, but Martha was busy, busy, busy. She was doing everything she *should* do, and that kept her running all the time.

But Jesus urged her to remember that "only one thing is needed." Keep the story of Martha in mind while I describe a much-too-busy existence I experienced.

The day I'm remembering started out as one of those mornings. You can almost hear the hurry-up-cartoon music in the background. . . .

I get up, get breakfast ready, make sure I haven't forgotten to make a lunch or check off the boys' school to-do list:

- *Sweet three-year-old Gabby needs a shoebox to make an Easter basket at school.*

- *And six-year-old Brooks has to remember show and tell.*

- *Oops, I almost forgot to include the permission slip for the field trip to the cookie factory.*

- *My six-month-old baby boy Garrett, with his big blue eyes and blond peach fuzz, can't seem to shake that cold.*

I call our pediatrician, who over the years has become a friend.

"Hello. No, nothing serious. Garrett has had the sniffles for more than a week now. OK, I'll bring him in just to make sure." Since he was the third child, I didn't rush to the doctor at the first sign of a sniffle anymore, but there was something about this cold I didn't like.

"All right guys, stop fighting over the last sausage; you'll have to split it. We have ten minutes to get out the door. Time to brush your teeth." While I bark orders like a drill sergeant, I pour what has become my morning inspiration on four hours of sleep.

Coffee . . . it's a vice, but a much-needed one, considering the week I'd had. I tried to do without the stuff, but I literally fell asleep at a red light once after dropping off the boys at school.

Why didn't I sleep? Well, that night when I got home from work at 11 P.M., there were dishes to do, things to pick up, and a project to catch up on. Finally after jumping into jammies and feeling like I might get to sleep . . . "Whaaaaaa!" It was baby Garrett. That cold was making him fussy and he couldn't sleep.

So, at midnight, it was time to rock-a-bye baby. Even though I was dead tired, it was a precious quiet moment with this little one. After an hour we both nodded off. I'm not sure who was drooling more, Garrett or Mom. "OK, little guy, back in the crib you go," I whispered.

Then Garrett responded, "Whaaaaa!" When I finally get him settled, it is 3:00 A.M. The boys get us up at 6:30 — I could still get three-and-a-half hours sleep. Something is better than nothing!

The next morning at the pediatrician, we were waiting in the exam room. I was playing with my little bald-headed, blue-eyed baby. He got so excited that he started kicking and thrashing and giggling while he was on the exam table. He was breathing a little heavy, but it was almost as if he were running in place. When the doctor walked in, she listened to him breathe . . . then listened again . . . and again. That's when I began to worry.

"He's breathing a little fast," she said. "I'd like to give him a breathing treatment and see what happens." My heart sank. My sweet beautiful little baby had something wrong? I didn't even think the fast breathing was a problem. He wasn't gasping for air, just breathing a little fast.

The doctor left the room, and a few minutes later a nurse brought in a strange-looking machine. "Here's how you do it," she said. She covered his nose with a cone-shaped piece of plastic attached to the machine. She poured a drug into a receptacle connected to the device. She said, "I'll be back," and then she left me on my own to cover my baby's nose and mouth with this contraption.

Awkwardly, I cradled little Garrett in my arms and pushed the nozzle to his nose. At first he looked at me as if to ask, *What's happening, Mom?* Then he screamed at the top of his lungs and cried bloody murder. That's when I felt weak. As my baby's tears rolled down his little face, my tears started rolling too. I couldn't imagine what must be going through his mind.

The doctor came back into the room, gently took the device off Garrett's face, and listened to his breathing. Then again, and then again.

"The treatment slowed his breathing down," she said. "While that's good, it shows that he needs the treatment. This could be a virus, or possibly the beginning of asthma. Let's do the treatments three times a day for a month. Then we'll see what happens."

The machine arrived at our home, and by the end of a month, his breathing seemed to be under control. After a few months of checkups, baby Garrett got a reprieve. His breathing seemed normal. He was OK, but my nerves had taken a beating. With the latest report of good health, though, the trouble was hopefully behind us.

Life continued at its normal chaotic pace. Like Martha in Luke 10, I found little time to thank God for each beautiful day, to listen to the birds sing in the morning, and to receive the gifts God had for me each day.

Little did I know that while I was battling my baby's health problem, I had a sneaky, deadly disease growing silently in my body—yet I felt fine. It was a cancer that would change how I looked at everything in my life.

REMOVING MY SUPERWOMAN CAPE

All cooks want to please their guests. Before you have company, don't you make sure you tidy up the house? Certainly, most of us want to provide a clean, comfortable setting for our visitors. You can see how God shaped my priorities.

Years ago, before the children, everything in the house had to be perfect. I would start to deep clean when I knew someone special was coming to visit. My focus would be the cleaning frenzy instead of the guest. I also focused on making the best meal ever! By the time my guest arrived, I would be exhausted! But true hospitality is to help make the guest feel welcome. It is easy to get caught up in the little stuff and lose perspective on your guest. It is also possible to get so caught up in the busy life that we lose perspective of God's plan for us.

While sitting in church one day, I realized I had filled my days too full with trying to be a good mom and not enough with listening to God. *I love being a mom!* My boys were so young and so active, and I constantly had to keep a close eye on them. As moms, we *are* called to focus on our children. But even parenting can cause us to get out of balance if we take our focus off of God and His

Word. I realized that day that I needed to take a step back and focus on what God had to say to me and how He wanted to mold me.

Think about the countless number of things we can place before God in our lives. Kids? Can it be a husband? Or maybe it's a job. Or perhaps it is the particular way we want to care for our families and manage our busy schedules overall. At one point in my life, I managed three boys' busy sports schedules, worked from home, and volunteered as classroom mom, Sunday school teacher, and team mom. These activities were so time consuming.

I have since realized that anything that takes our attention and focus away from putting God first can be a pitfall. In Exodus 20:3, God commands that we should have no other gods besides Him. With all of these other activities, it is easy to end up focusing on the wrong thing. Am I superwoman? God has shown me that I need to hang up that mythical cape. He alone is all-powerful.

Are you allowing a busy life to rule you and be your god? Are you rushing through life and missing all of God's blessings? Or breaking out of being a type A!? God does not intend for us to be stressed and full of anxiety. In fact, we know worry can be considered a sin. When we worry, we are not exercising faith. But that is a common state of being for many of us these days.

How can we find time to listen to the Lord and put aside being busy? Getting up a few minutes earlier to worship may allow that precious intimate time with Jesus. Where can you find time in your day to spend with Jesus?

 Surrender your worries, cares, and hurts to God in prayer.

Our Key Scripture

"God is faithful and reliable. If we confess our sins, he forgives them and cleanses us from everything we've done wrong" (1 JOHN 1:9 GWT).

Storms from Sin

HIDDEN SIN

There was an adorable child on YouTube. He had naughtily eaten a treat before dinner. He had the cake crumbs and icing all over his little mouth. When his mom repeatedly asked him if he'd eaten the treat, he repeatedly said no. He even threw in a, "Why don't you believe me?!" It was hilarious. But it goes to prove that it's human nature to hide from sin.

In spite of that natural tendency of ours, the truth is that God is all knowing and all seeing; we can't hide our problems or sins. If you ignore cancer, a relationship, or your depleted bank account, it will only get worse. Put it in the light and deal with it.

Adam and Eve certainly tried. The Lord God took the man and put him in the Garden of Eden to work it and take care of it.

"And the LORD God commanded the man, 'You are free to eat from any tree in the garden; but you must not eat from the tree of the knowledge of good and evil, for when you eat from it you will certainly die'" (Genesis 2:16–17).

"'You will not certainly die,' the serpent said to the woman. 'For God knows that when you eat from it your eyes will be opened, and you will be like God, knowing good and evil.' When the woman saw that the fruit of the tree was good for food and pleasing to the eye, and also desirable for gaining wisdom, she took some and ate it. She also gave some to her husband, who was with her, and he ate it.

"Then the eyes of both of them were opened, and they realized they were naked; so they sewed fig leaves together and made coverings for themselves. Then the man and his wife heard the sound of the LORD God as he was walking in the garden in the cool of the day, and they hid from the LORD God among the trees of the garden. But the LORD God called to the man, 'Where are you?' He answered, 'I heard you in the garden, and I was afraid because I was naked; so I hid.'

"And he said, 'Who told you that you were naked? Have you eaten from the tree that I commanded you not to eat from?' The man said, 'The woman you put here with me—she gave me some fruit from the tree, and I ate it.' Then the LORD God said to the woman, 'What is this you have done?' The woman said, 'The serpent deceived me, and I ate'" (Genesis 3:4–13).

Adam and Eve were hiding from God. Their eyes were open. But instead of admitting it, they tried to hide from it. And they passed that propensity down to all of their offspring, including you and me.

God promises that when we confess sin to Him, he will help us mightily. And the Lord doesn't want you to ignore someone's sin against you and just cover it up. In that case it will only fester. If we don't fess up to those around us that we might have offended, then our relationship problems can't be fixed. My infamous home disaster illustrated that very clearly.

Earlier I told you how a leaky refrigerator caused major damage in our house. That water leak no doubt started slowly and then busted loose, wreaking havoc with the wood floors and subfloors. That water got in between the grain and distorted the wood. Because it wasn't exposed and dealt with, it weakened the wood to the point where the bad stuff had to be cut out.

So let's compare the damaged wood rot or decay in a tooth to what sin does to us. In a house or in a mouth, decay can lead to loss. Obviously in a tooth a dentist has to cut out or drill away the decay. In a house, wood that becomes wet and damaged leads to rot and decay too. Again, you have to cut out the bad stuff, repair it, and then rebuild it with new material.

Sin gets into the crevices of our heart and tears us down. Sin can also do the same to our relationships with others and ultimately erode our relationship with God. Does something in your past still hurt? Have you exposed it and admitted it is there? Then have you asked God to remove it and renew you?

God loves us so much that He has designed an easy-to-understand way to reconnect with Him. Simply confess sin to the Lord and ask for forgiveness. Ask the person we are in conflict with to forgive us. Then stop beating ourselves up, and accept our sweet Lord's forgiveness. That's how we can truly cut the wood rot or decay (sin) out of our heart.

Then, just like the move-out crew, we can move out things that cause sin in life. Maybe it's anger, jealousy, putting other things ahead of God, or maybe it's simply not trusting God enough. Perhaps it's something we're doing, or a show we watch on TV. Is it putting something or someone where God should be? Is it fear?

Not trusting God by living in fear shows a lack of faith and is considered a sin. Let's take time now to list it here and then call on Jesus to move it out like the move-out crew.

Cut sin and pain out of your life, just as the demolition crew removed the damaged wood. Allow the forgiveness to flow, and let healing begin.

By the way, that move-out crew was amazing. They came to put the furniture and everything sitting on the kitchen floor, dining room floor, office floor, and living room floor into a storage pod. The amazing part of this process was that some of the crew members were expert organizers. They packed and unpacked, and the place never looked better. Everything inside cabinets and drawers was stacked perfectly.

I chuckled because I remember praying for the Lord to help me get organized. I just had no idea He would use a leaky refrigerator to help me accomplish that. That's how God can work through our lives! He can remove the bad stuff that gets into the crevices of our souls. The things that hurt can get in our head and become worse over time. Just as He cleaned up and restored my home after my mishap, we need to let Him clean up and restore us.

UNFORGIVENESS

"And forgive us our debts, as we forgive our debtors" (Matthew 6:12 KJV). "Forgive us our sins" (Luke 11:4). Our sin causes our debt. We fall under Satan's control when we give into sin. But Jesus paid with His blood so that we could be free! So if we are forgiven, then what must we do for others? *We must forgive those in our lives, just as He has forgiven us.*

It hurts, it stings, and the human reaction is to lash back, to punch back, to want to hurt them back! That's how wars start, that's how lifelong friends separate for good.

We tell on the news that a gang member was shot and killed because someone else had shot or killed a member of a rival gang. Revenge is not gratifying. Revenge is not healing to the spirit. The thought of revenge feeds the ulcerated sore in a wounded spirit.

The Lord blessed us with the ability to speak. Our words can be life giving or demeaning. They can literally crush a spirit. "The soothing tongue is a tree of life, but a perverse tongue crushes the spirit" (Proverbs 15:4). God tells us that we can do anything under His power. "I can do all things through Christ who strengthens me" (Philippians 4:13 KJV). He tells us that, with the power of the Holy Spirit, we can heal.

"Do not take revenge, my dear friends, but leave room for God's wrath, for it is written: 'It is mine to avenge; I will repay,' says the Lord" (Romans 12:19). As much as we might want to take matters into our own hands to get justice for a wrongdoing, the Lord clearly tells us to turn the hurt, pain, and injustice over to Him. We can relax in knowing we have a great, big God, and He has our back.

We don't have to be the judge and jury. God sees all, including the injustices, and He will deal with those who sin against us and Him. So turn it over to the Lord and heal from hurt. "For God will bring every deed into judgment, including every hidden thing, whether it is good or evil" (Ecclesiastes 12:14).

Forgive, so that you are forgiven. Forgiveness is for the other person, but it is more powerful for you and your health, especially your spiritual health! No grumbling . . . it is gone!

> *"Therefore I tell you, whatever you ask for in prayer, believe that you have received it, and it will be yours. And when you stand praying, if you hold anything against anyone, forgive them, so that your father in heaven may forgive you your sins"* (Mark 11:24–25).

It's simple math: forgiveness = freedom!

Carolyn Mckinstry has an amazing story of forgiveness. She had been in the Sixteenth Street Baptist Church when it was bombed in 1963. Just before the blast, she opened the bathroom door in the basement of the church to remind the girls it was time to get to the service. Moments later, the blast exploded that rocked the world and changed the civil rights movement. During an interview, she told me, "I had to forgive for me . . . replace the hate with love!"

It's all about priorities. What's most important in life? To be upset over something that's broken, or to forgive? King David wrote, "You, LORD, are forgiving and good, abounding in love to all who call to you" (Psalm 86:5). We need to act the same way. Feel the blessing of a loving, forgiving heart. Be generous in forgiving transgressions. It is a great feeling to truly forgive someone you know does not deserve it.

We as sinners don't deserve the Lord's grace, but He gives it freely if we just ask Him for it. It is nothing we earn, it's free! It is a choice. God gave us free will. Each day we can choose what is better, or choose to be at the mercy of life. We can become mature in Him.

IMPATIENCE

I love children's parties at parks. It was a perfect October day. Not too hot, not too cold, it was just right. My oldest son was six years old. He was attending his buddy's sixth birthday party. They all ran and climbed on the playground equipment.

A game of tag finished the festivities for the day. Then it was time for the pet shop demonstration. Yes: rats, mice, snakes, and lizards. All the things little boys love. The closing ceremonies to these grand-event birthdays always included an enthusiastic "Happy Birthday" song before children would dive into the chocolate birthday cake with a plastic lizard on it.

Yes, it was a perfect day, until we got the party gift. The child's mom was keeping with the theme from the pet store, right down to the party gift—a fish. That's right, a little goldfish. I was so shocked that I felt my jaw drop. I forced my limp, lower mouth into a smile and said, "Wow, thank you. Look, Brooks, you got a fish!"

He came running over to me and grabbed the bag and started to shake it like it was shake-and-bake chicken! I didn't know a lot about fish, but I figured 10.5 on the Richter scale couldn't be good for anyone. So I told him to stop that.

All the way home, Brooks was yapping about his fish, while I was thinking *who in the world would give a fish as a party gift?* We put the bag with the little finned wonder on the kitchen counter, overnight, and just as I feared, he was floating upside down by morning. Brooks ran into the kitchen to say good morning to the fish. He asked if it was OK. I said sure, and I would ask the pet store about it. Then Brooks, satisfied with the answer, trotted off to go to school.

Later that morning I packed up the limp floating fish and marched right back to the pet store. When I held up the body, he said, "OK, we will trade it in." *Oh good*, I thought, still steamed that I had a fish forced on us. But it had died, and now I was realizing that I have to get this new fish a companion. After all, *wouldn't it be cruel for a fish to swim around alone for the rest of his little life?*

Then the slick salesman convinces me I need a bigger tank than just a small bowl. Of course I "need" the little colored stones, filter, scooper, etc., etc., etc. More than $100 later I am walking out with two fish and a bunch of stuff I don't want! I felt like I had been bamboozled.

And about a month later, guess what happened to those little gold beauties I paid so handsomely for. That's right! They died. Being a fixer, I scooped them up and gave them a proper send off in the hopper. This happened all before I heard the pitter-patter of Brooks's little feet.

Soon after I dumped the fish bodies, little Brooks stepped into the kitchen. I put my biggest happy face on. "Good morning, honey!" I *hoped* he wouldn't spot the empty fish tank, but I *knew* he would. Each and every day since the little creatures swam into our lives, he had tapped on the glass of the tank and said good morning to them.

Brooks said, "Where's Goldy and Sam?"

Oh no! What do I say? Then, thinking fast, I said, "Goldy and Sam swam through the pipes to visit their Uncle Herman. Uhh . . . ," I stammered, "Don't worry, they'll be back." Then I thought, *Did I really say that?!?!* Ugh.

After taking him to school, I headed back to the pet godfather. Why do I call him that? Because he reminds me of the line in the *Godfather III* movie where Al Pacino commented about trying to get out of the Mafia, "Just when you think you're out, they suck you back in!"

I was being suckered back in to being a fish owner. I could have been brave. I could have told Brooks the fish died and used it as a life lesson. After all, death is a part of life. I could have asked God how to use that as a teaching moment. I could have sat back and let go and let God. But I was chicken and impatiently decided what to do rather than wait on God and let Him handle it differently.

It's one of my many life lessons: learning to have more patience, learning to wait for God.

DISOBEDIENCE

In life, we need to know the rules. If we try to plunge into something without knowing the rules, we can end up failing, or even getting hurt.

One Sunday we were in church and missing one of our boys. Our oldest son had spent the night with a friend and was meeting us at church. It happened to be April Fool's Day, so I was just waiting for the boys to prank me.

When I spotted Brooks with his arm in a sling wrapped in what looked like miles of gauze, I started laughing hysterically! I said, "Good one, Brooks. Haha! Oh, I guess I should gasp and say, 'Oh no, what happened to you? Wow, what a prank! Haha!'"

But he looked puzzled at my reaction. About that time, the mom of the boy whom my ten-year-old had stayed with ran up to me with an apologetic expression on her face. She said, "I am so sorry that Brooks got hurt. We let him ride the dirt bike, and apparently he didn't know where the brakes were."

They were dead serious. He really was hurt! But mainly just scratches and bruises. Big bruises! Before riding anything, make sure you know where the brakes are. In life, God gives us His Word for instruction, to tell us how to proceed, when and how to slow down, and when to stop. "Listen to my instruction and be wise; do not disregard it" (Proverbs 8:33).

ENVY AND COMPLAINING

I remember looking at a friend and thinking, *wow, she has a great life.* I was envious that she seemed to have it all, and more. Within a few months, I was shocked to learn that she and her husband were getting a divorce.

Then it hit me between the eyes: everyone has to deal with something sooner or later in their lives. Seeing my friend's divorce gave my little storms some perspective. I like to look at problems as if they are boulders. If you allow that problem, or boulder, to remain in front of you, it's hard to see where your path is heading. It becomes overwhelming and daunting. Remember the saying, "You are making a mountain out of a mole hill!"

> *"Do everything without complaining or arguing, so that you may become blameless and pure, children of God without fault in a crooked and depraved generation, in which you shine like stars in the universe as you hold out the word of life — in order that I may boast on the day of Christ that I did not run or labor for nothing. But even if I am being poured out like a drink offering on the sacrifice and service coming from your faith, I am glad and rejoice with all of you. So you too should be glad and rejoice with me"* (Philippians 2:14–18).

The Lord is personal. He knows our human nature is to complain—especially when we are tired. I get tired from trying to do too much. Just like Martha, I start out with great intentions to make a great meal. But then that leaves dirty dishes, which means the kitchen needs cleaning. But then the rest of the house looks dirty compared to the kitchen. Halfway through, I get tired and start complaining that no one is helping me.

Reread the passage from Philippians 2, and contemplate the direction to do everything without complaining. This is a command that will help us be more like Christ. Remember, Jesus did not complain, even when He was hanging on the Cross. He even prayed for the men who were causing His torture.

Keep in mind that we might be the only glimpse someone has of what it is to be a Christian. You are a representative of the King. Complaining about trivial matters might just discourage others from seeking salvation. Complaining and being discontented with God's will are expressions of unbelief. Is there an area of life you would like to change?

ANGER

My husband of 13 years, Doug, saw me at my worst and lowest points after my surgery. He was constantly coming home with stories of hope and survival. He saw me cry, and he held me in his arms to comfort me. When I asked if he could still love me, he reassured me. God sent this man to be my partner. There were times in our marriage that I needed to be there for him, and now I needed him to be there for me.

He said all the right things the week after surgery. I feel like I was in shock for weeks, but then there was the next emotion to deal with—anger. I never actually got angry at God, but there were times when I did have unexplained anger. Little things would bring feelings of rage. If I dropped something, it might make me really mad. I later realized that I wasn't really mad about that particular event; it was all just part of the healing process. I would get mad about something so insignificant that it would make me shake my own head at myself.

For example, after I had returned to work and tried to get my life back to normal, I was left out of the planning for a school party. I knew logically that I'd been out of the loop because of my illness. People probably had thought I was too weak to help. They were actually being thoughtful. But I was ready to reclaim my role as Mommy. I was angry over nothing.

When I'd go for my daily walk, I'd feel anger well up inside me. I had no particular reason to feel that way, but it was there. I knew I was angry that I had cancer. I wasn't angry at anyone; I was just *angry*. Walking and praying and talking helped.

I consulted with my friend Lisa Baggett about the anger. She had been a counselor, and she assured me that it was normal. Her son had been stricken with a benign brain tumor, and for a long time after that crisis, she felt pangs of anger that it had happened to him. Even after successful surgery to remove the tumor, she still had to deal with that emotion.

Immediately after my diagnosis, Doug would urge me not to cry. He wanted me to be happy and strong. But as Dr. Winchester reminded him, crying is good for the immune system. After that, he'd look at me and say, "Is this one of those moments?" I'd say, "Yes, honey, I'm having a moment."

The word *moment* spoke volumes in our home. It meant that this was a time I needed for myself to cry and deal with what was happening in my life. "Yes, I just need one right now," I'd say. Then he'd hug me. I knew he wanted to make it all go away. He wanted to make it all better. I wanted him to make it go away, too, but

I knew he couldn't. The only thing he could do was allow me to have that "moment" and stand by me and let me know he was there.

I can also tell you there was plenty of laughter. Sometimes what was happening to me seemed so ridiculous that Doug and I would just break down and laugh. That, too, became a great way to release tension. He'd call me "baldy." I'd lightly slap him and we'd both laugh. The chiding was welcomed. I knew that if he was kidding me, I must really be OK. My doctor encouraged laughter; that's also good for the immune system.

Bald jokes ran rampant in our house. I really had fun with him when I turned the tables and pretended to find a bald spot on the top of *his* head. I never saw a man go running for a hand-held mirror so fast in my life! He wasn't really going bald, but for a brief second he understood how I felt. Being able to laugh at myself and the whole situation really helped.

I know Doug went through a lot of emotional changes. But even though he had turmoil inside, he always tried to remain calm and be my strong Rock of Gibraltar. While women reach out to others for help, it's not always that easy for men to admit they need help. His story hopefully will help other men who are going through the same thing to not feel so alone.

I told Doug that I knew I was overreacting to some things, but I knew that it had something to do the emotions of a cancer diagnosis. He always understood. I finally asked the Lord to take the anger away. I had no room in my life for it anymore. After all, I was trying very hard to enjoy every day.

Doug supported me through that time when I was an argument waiting to happen. He was patient and kind. He didn't always understand why I was upset, but he knew that I was working through the process of coming to grips with the fact that I had cancer.

Sometimes even the things he said to try to help would lead me to tears. I wanted him to fix everything for me.

But I don't have to be angry about it anymore. Through my tears, I came to a wonderful revelation. Jesus is perfect, but the rest of us sometimes say and do the wrong things. That's OK; we are human. But with the Lord's guidance, we can get back on track and stay there.

 What patience and guidance can God provide for you?

Our Key Scripture

"Our Father, who art in heaven, Hallowed be thy Name. Thy kingdom come. Thy will be done, On earth as it is in heaven. Give us this day our daily bread. And forgive us our trespasses, As we forgive those who trespass against us. And lead us not into temptation, But deliver us from evil. For thine is the kingdom, and the power, and the glory, for ever and ever. Amen" (MATTHEW 6:9–13 KJV).

CHAPTER 5

Facing Storms with Prayer

POWERFUL PRAYER

The greatest teacher of prayer is our Savior. Jesus prayed about everything. He prayed at His own baptism from John (Luke 3:21). He prayed as He chose the Apostles (Luke 6:12). He prayed on the Cross. The very last words before His death were in prayer (Luke 23:46).

His disciples saw that He prayed, and they wanted to know how He did it. That's how we got the "Lord's Prayer" (Luke 11:1–4), which teaches us not only *what* to pray about what, but also what order to pray things *in*.

By calling Him "Our Father," we remind ourselves that He is close to and intimate with us. Then, by turning to Him as God in heaven, we acknowledge Him as the Supreme Ruler of the universe. Also, in claiming to be His children, we remember that we are related to each other as brothers and sisters in Christ. We are in a spiritual family, the body of Christ, and we are united with the Lord and angels as we pray. Therefore, we pray for not only ourselves, but for all people. We need to ask for God's goodness for others.

By praying "Hallowed be thy name," we ask that His name might be Holy for all people, that everyone might glorify the name of God by their words and deeds. With "Thy Kingdom come," we keep in mind that the kingdom of God begins within a believer, when the grace of God, having filled him, cleanses and transfigures his inner world. And by mentioning His kingdom, we also put into words our hope of a new world someday that will be ruled by Him.

When you pray, you are connecting with the kingdom of God! When we say, "Thy will be done, on earth as it is in heaven," we are desiring that everything in the world be done for the good and glory of God. We should do God's work here on earth. That is a slice of heaven. We are His hands. We can show people what His kingdom looks like through our actions. When you help others, you help yourself!

You can see that by following the order of Jesus' instructions for prayer, almost immediately any storms we have come to talk to Him about seem less daunting. And we are directed to pray all of this before we ask for our first piece of "daily bread"!

Another lesson Jesus gave us about prayer was when He knew He was about to be crucified. He knew it would be painful in so many ways. He knew He could talk to His Father about anything. We can take any concern to Him. But Jesus teaches us that, although God always answers prayers, sometimes God's answer has to be no. Just like we as parents sometimes have to say no to our children—for their good, of course.

Then Jesus went with his disciples to a place called
Gethsemane, and he said to them, "Sit here while I

go over there and pray." He took Peter and the two sons of Zebedee along with him, and he began to be sorrowful and troubled. Then he said to them, "My soul is overwhelmed with sorrow to the point of death. Stay here and keep watch with me."

Going a little farther, he fell with his face to the ground and prayed, "My Father, if it is possible, may this cup be taken from me. Yet not as I will, but as you will." Then he returned to his disciples and found them sleeping. "Couldn't you men keep watch with me for one hour?" He asked Peter. "Watch and pray so that you will not fall into temptation. The spirit is willing, but the flesh is weak." He went away a second time and prayed, "My Father, if it is not possible for this cup to be taken away unless I drink it, may your will be done" (Matthew 26:36–42).

Jesus was praying this for our benefit. He even said that the reason He came down here to earth was to die for our sins and redeem us for Himself. "Now my soul is troubled, and what shall I say? 'Father, save me from this hour'? No, it was for this very reason I came to this hour" (John 12:27). Of course He wasn't going to abandon His mission at the last minute.

But even though the Father didn't take the cup of the Cross away from His Son, He raised Him from the dead, saving all those whom Jesus died for. Jesus loves love, and there's nothing greater that He could do for us than give Himself. "Greater love has no one than this: to lay down one's life for one's friends" (John 15:13).

Plus, Jesus will get *us*, His Bride! Listen to the excitement in the Lord's voice as He describes getting to spend eternity with us:

> *"The voice of joy, and the voice of gladness, the voice of the bridegroom, and the voice of the bride, the voice of them that shall say, Praise the LORD of hosts: for the LORD is good; for his mercy endures forever"* (Jeremiah 33:11 KJV).

Even more directly, Jesus said "Father, I want those you have given me to be with me where I am" (John 17:24). We are encouraged to be happy about what He did for us. "Let us rejoice and be glad and give him glory! For the wedding of the Lamb has come, and his bride has made herself ready" (Revelation 19:7).

Praying is a personal and intimate time with the Lord. He is sweet, kind, and loving. We each can spend personal time with Him in prayer.

> *"And when you pray, do not be like the hypocrites, for they love to pray standing in the synagogues and on the street corners to be seen by others. Truly I tell you, they have received their reward in full. But when you pray, go into your room, close the door and pray to your Father, who is unseen. Then your Father, who sees what is done in secret, will reward you"* (Matthew 6:5–6).

And the best thing is that He answers! "I will instruct you and teach you in the way you should go; I will counsel you with my loving eye on you" (Psalm 32:8). When I pray, the Lord directs me in *every* aspect of life—from parenting, to personal relationships, to business.

Some days I go to work simply to do my job. But sometimes I go to work and I see God in action. I am blown away by how His answers to prayer can set the wheels in motion for us to help each other. Remember that we are called to be the hands and feet of Christ. We are called to use our gifts, talents, and abilities to help point others to Christ.

There is power in prayer. Pray for yourself, your family, and even for people who hurt you. "But I tell you, love your enemies and pray for those who persecute you" (Matthew 5:44). Pray for all of the children, for their safety in schools, malls, and in all public places. Pray that evil deeds are exposed. Pray for forgiveness. Pray for the homeless. Pray for our leaders. In other words, pray about everything! "Don't worry about anything; instead, pray about everything. Tell God what you need, and thank him for all he has done" (Philippians 4:6 NLT).

VICTORY ON DEATH ROW

In one hot week in July, God showed me not one—but three—stories of prayer that were connected to baseball.

The first story happened to me. I had prayed for my well-deserved, upcoming week of vacation to be a good one. My 19-year-old son, Brooks, had come home from college for the summer. He had taken the summer off and come home to intern at the local Birmingham Barons baseball team. But he brought to my attention that he needed sinus surgery. So, instead of fluttering off to a Gulf Coast beach or some exotic destination, I became Nurse Mom while he recovered.

Our floors that were being demolished were under construction that same week, and my husband the sportscaster was off somewhere broadcasting a golf tournament. So the boys and I took up residence upstairs. It was a week in which we enjoyed a number of movies. I cherished the time. Spending that much time with them was becoming a rarity. I knew that, in just a matter of weeks, Brooks would go back to college in Alabama. The Lord knew what was best for me—for us.

The second baseball story showed up when we all went to watch a local Little League game. An 11-year-old boy on the mound kept bending over, seeming to touch his shoe each time he faced a new batter. The other boys couldn't figure out what he was doing. The parents couldn't figure it out either. Someone offered that perhaps he has a bad shoelace?

Finally my son Garrett couldn't stand it anymore. When the boy came in to the dugout to get ready to bat, Garrett asked him, "What are you doing bending over all the time?"

The boy simply responded, "Praying!"

He had it right. We are told to pray without ceasing. That means having a daily, ongoing dialogue with our Lord.

The third story came to me just after I'd returned to work from my unglamorous vacation. My next assignment was to interview a Christian comedienne. I contacted Mrs. V, and within

20 seconds she had replied, saying that she would be happy to do the interview. In fact, she was ecstatic.

Mrs. V arrived, absolutely stunning in a bright green dress. She is a tall, beautiful lady. Her huge smile lit up the room. She was with her handsome husband, Edward. I thought to myself, *Well, they really have it made. They must have a fun life.*

But when I asked why she wanted to make people laugh, we got on the subject of tough times. She told me she had lost her oldest daughter to a playground accident. She explained that she wants to encourage and empower other women, to help them heal from pain in their lives.

We talked about how God uses tough times in our lives to help us grow. As if on cue, she pointed to her husband. She said, "Edward, for example, was on death row in prison." My head turned to look at him so fast I almost got whiplash. He said, "Yes, I was."

As the Lord continued weaving in His baseball theme, Edward explained that he had played college ball. In fact, he had been so talented that his college coach contacted some professional scouts. But he said he had grown too tired of watching his mother struggle. He didn't want to wait to finish college, play in the minor leagues, and then hope he'd make it to the majors and get a big contract. He wanted some big money right away.

Drug dealers can sense that kind of desperation, and he was soon lured in by them. He wanted the expensive car and clothes, so he began to sell. He quickly worked his way into an influential position.

When three people were gunned down in his territory, the police went after Edward. Although he didn't commit the murders, he was arrested. Full of pride, he told a police officer that he'd be out in less than 24 hours. He was not. But he says the most hurtful thing was when he had to face his mother.

The first time she came to see him in prison, she brought a letter with her. It was from the Atlanta Braves. They had invited him to Spring Training Camp. If he had not been incarcerated, his dream of playing professional baseball would have unfolded. He braced himself to hear the words he knew she'd speak: "You couldn't have waited for *this?*" He knew right then that he'd have probably been able to have the life he had wanted, if he had just stayed away from the drugs and continued to play ball.

Edward eventually ended up on death row. Even though his lawyer worked tirelessly to get him off, Edward hit the lowest point of his life. In one last effort to find hope, he called his high-school sweetheart, Valencia. She immediately started praying with him on the phone, and she'd pray every time he called. Then she went to visit him in prison. Between Valencia's prayers and his lawyer's appeals, Edward got moved from death row, to life in prison, and then finally to being paroled.

Edward now is committed to talking to young people, warning them not to take the path he took. The Holy Spirit helped turn Edward's life around!

> *"I pray that out of his glorious riches he may strengthen you with power through his Spirit in your inner being, so that Christ may dwell in your hearts through faith. And I pray that you, being rooted and established in love, may have power, together with all the Lord's holy*

people, to grasp how wide and long and high and deep is the love of Christ, and to know this love that surpasses knowledge — that you may be filled to the measure of all the fullness of God. Now to him who is able to do immeasurably more than all we ask or imagine, according to his power that is at work within us, to him be glory in the church and in Christ Jesus throughout all generations, for ever and ever! Amen" (Ephesians 3:16–21).

SOMETIMES NO, SOMETIMES YES

Prayer doesn't exclusively have to be applied to life-and-death situations. But, as Momma always said, "Be careful what you pray for and ask for, you just might get it." This was something that always perplexed me. "If I ask for something, Mom, why wouldn't I want it? If it came my way, what's the harm?"

I have to admit, I have a tendency to be a frustrated eater. I recognize that I need to be leaning on God during my frustrations and not on chocolate chip cookies. I said a prayer asking God to help me to trust Him more and lean on sweets less.

But then came the day when 14 years of my life were packed up and put into temporary pods (because most of our downstairs floors were ruined by that refrigerator leak), followed by other day-to-day challenges, that I reached for a bag of sugar-free gummy bears. I pushed out of my head the distant memory about the upset stomach I'd contracted the last time I had eaten sugar-free candy. I didn't really think that there was a connection. So I ate and ate and ate these gummy bears. Yes, I ate a lot of them. The soft, chewy consistency somehow helped temporarily melt away the frustrations of the day.

Not surprisingly, within 30 minutes, my stomach started rumblin' and tumblin'. It was major upset. Curiosity made me reach for the empty gummy bear bag to try to find out what ingredient could possibly have thrown my stomach into such turmoil. There it was, on the bottom of the back of the package, "Caution: some people with an artificial-sweetener sensitivity may experience a laxative effect. That was it! Thank You, Lord, for curing me from reaching for food to deal with chaos. Lean on God!

The Lord can also inject humor into prayer. Years ago I was speaking at a missionary conference, and our entire family took a Jeep ride in Sedona, Arizona! All five of us—my husband, three boys and I—were strapped in as a guide drove us over rough, steep terrain.

Garrett was only three years old. We had talked a lot recently about how God is with us during a crisis. He had seen me pray during my cancer battle. But I didn't know if my baby boy really understood going to God in a crisis until we were bouncing through the desert. It was frighteningly bumpy at times, and for a three-year-old, it was probably a terrifying experience.

I looked over at the little guy, who had his hands together as we bumped along. I heard him say, "Word, Word, save me Word, save me, Word!" He couldn't say the *L* in *Lord*, but he was praying his best, turning to God when he was scared. Good boy. Praise God!

Just like Garrett, I go to God whenever. But during the scary times, I find myself praying even more. When fear creeps into your life, do you reach for prayer and not the gummies? During my cancer battle I found myself praying constantly. And I saw God working and responding to each prayer.

When I was diagnosed with cancer, I prayed for the diagnosis to have been a mistake. From the time I heard the news of my positive biopsy, until I had the surgery to remove it, I prayed that the cancer would just melt away on its own. I was in my bathroom on my knees begging for God to take it away. But even though I could almost feel His fatherly arms around me, I knew the answer was no.

I could feel the Lord saying that this was a journey I had to go on. I could feel Him assuring me that He would be with me every step of the way. I literally felt the same as when I really wanted something and my parents said no. It was the feeling of having a door shut in your face. As a reporter, I was trained to never take no for an answer. But if it's God saying no, then I'm good with that. *Your will, not mine Lord. Your will, not mine.*

When there are troubles, I tend to brace myself. Then my mind races to try to figure out how to fix the problem. Then when I realize how ill-equipped I am to "fix it," I lay the problem at my Father's feet.

Many times I prayed for healing from the cancer. There are times when I have prayed for my parents' healing from different maladies. I have prayed for the healing of my family and friends. But each time, once I lay the worry at my Father's feet, that's when I see His loving and powerful force at work. I've seen both bodies and relationships healed. But it is only after I finally lay it down.

Just imagine a little girl holding her favorite doll. She is crying because her doll is torn. You offer to take a look to see if you can help by sewing it. But even though she wants it fixed, she clenches the doll even tighter. She won't turn it over to the person who could fix it.

I feel like that little girl quite often. But the Lord has been teaching me that when I really turn it over, He can put the pieces together, wipe away the tears, and restore joy! The power of prayer can't be explained scientifically. It can't be measured, and it can't be calculated in a mathematical equation. I know this intimately.

Many years ago I received a phone call that was a blow to my heart. It was my mom. She told me that she was going blind! A fall had apparently injured the back of both of her retinas. It was a progressive blindness. She was told that her sight would diminish day by day until there was nothing but blackness.

My stomach felt sick because of the news. I was so upset I could not sleep that night. My head was spinning as I tried to figure out why this was happening to one of the sweetest people in the world! And anger was rising inside of me at the injustice of it all. It was not fair!

So I did all that I knew how to do, and that was pray. I prayed intensely. I prayed all night, literally until the sun came up. Now God instructs us that we don't have to keep repeating the request, but somehow praying all night seemed to help me with the grief I felt.

Later that morning, I called to check on her. She asked if I had prayed for her the previous night, because she said she felt so. She was unsure whether she had dreamed this, but there was one time she'd heard the words of someone praying for her. She had even sat up in bed. She also felt a heat around her eyes.

She was not healed instantly, by any means, but five eye surgeries later, and against all odds, she could see, and the progression of the blindness had stopped. Praise God!

I believe in the power of prayer! I know I shouldn't be surprised when God answers a prayer in a very real way, but I often feel in awe.

Learn to let go of your worry, go to the Lord in prayer, and surrender whatever burdens you. "Can any one of you by worrying add a single hour to your life?" (Matthew 6:27).

Worry will never solve anything, nor will it help solve a problem. God is power in action in our lives. He tells us to turn our cares and anxiety over to Him. "Rejoice always, pray continually, give thanks in all circumstances; for this is God's will for you in Christ Jesus" (1 Thessalonians 5:16–18). Have you prayed and asked God to show you His will in your life? If not, you can do so right now.

PRAYER WORKS, IN TIME

Can prayer change things? Yes. Can prayer change minds? Yes. I have experienced God's miracles in praying for people whom I thought would never change their minds.

Sitting in the driveway after my first positive cancer diagnosis, I was confiding in my husband that I was going to look into this cancer thing and be the first person to figure out why I ended up with it. *Look out world*. I thought I should tell everyone about my story and warn others about cancer.

I'm not sure what made me think I could figure it out in a few days. I would have been wasting my time, considering there are a few thousand researchers in labs who have spent decades trying to figure out cancer. I learned that I simply had to trust God.

The second time I was diagnosed, I wasn't so strong. I threw a hissy fit! I think it was almost worse, because I knew what I was facing. I *didn't* want cancer again. I *didn't* want surgery. I *didn't* want chemo.

But I then reached up once again and said, "I can't do this alone, I need you, Lord."

> *"But they that wait upon the* LORD *shall renew their strength; they shall mount up with wings as eagles; they shall run, and not be weary; and they shall walk, and not faint"* (Isaiah 40:31 KJV).

When we wait on God, amazing things happen, even in the midst of waiting for what we consider a long time.

More than 20 years ago, on a sunny spring morning, I remember the dedication to the first house opening for Grace House Ministries. The mayor was there, along with board members and volunteers. The girls stood beside Mama Lois Coleman as she prayed to bless the home, the girls, and the community. It was such a powerful prayer; I remember it to this day.

She prayed to reclaim the community of Fairfield, Alabama, for the Lord. At that time, there were many rundown homes and suspected crack houses. She said we are in a spiritual battle here, and we claim this land in the name of the Lord.

I was reminded of that prayer when my 13-year-old Garrett said we needed to go to Fairfield for our serve day. It's a thrift store set up by the church to help provide food and clothes to those in need. We are cleaning up the building for them so that the people can shop in a clean, pleasant place.

I thought, *Well, Lord, You are answering that prayer from more than 20 years ago.* It is a Christian thrift store where the workers are also called to minister to the needs of the people. Restoration Academy also was born in Fairfield in the last decade. It is a private Christian School. Many of the children are Grace House girls or children whom the community sponsored to attend there.

Grace House and a church started a community garden where for just ten dollars, people can pick all the vegetables they wish throughout the summer. The ministry has grown from serving 3 girls to 24. It has also purchased more houses along Farrell Avenue. The home and Mama Lois offer the children in Fairfield a weekly Bible study and much-needed food.

Yes, prayers to reclaim Fairfield for the Lord are being answered, and our own personal prayers will be too. Sometimes it just takes a little time, and then maybe a little bit more.

Our Key Scripture

"Hold on to instruction, do not let it go; guard it well, for it is your life"
(Proverbs 4:13).

Staying Strong in the Storm

ADMIT SIN

Before we can move from the difficulties of the storms into the encouraging times, we need to not only remove barriers that stand between the Lord and us, but we need to also keep our eyes focused on Him and His Word. The Lord showed me this recently in a metaphor that hit close to home, literally.

Yes, I'm talking about that refrigerator leak again. It created such damage in our kitchen and living room you would have thought Niagara Falls had busted loose in our home. The water ruined the floor, the subfloor, and the sub-sub . . . whatever is beneath that. It ruined our wood floor in the living room, dining room, and office. It ruined the pantry and the wall behind the fridge. In other words it was a bit of a mess! Thank the good Lord for insurance.

But that life disruption was a reminder that focusing on the Lord is better than focusing on the chaos of life. Walking into the kitchen was like walking into a war zone. The tile floor had been chipped away to reveal water-damaged wood. The water had left a black stain on the wood. In fact, the water weakened the wood so badly that when I stepped on it, it felt like it was going to collapse.

The damaged, putrid part had to be cut completely out. The workers cut two big sections out of the kitchen floor. You could see right through to the crawl space below. It reminded me of how sin in our lives can make us weak and tear apart our relationships and lives. Sin also deteriorates our relationship with our Lord and Savior. Apart from God's Word, our lives are filled with storms that cause dangerous leaks. With His instruction, we can face our storms and stay focused on Him.

> *"And you forgave the guilt of my sin. Therefore let all the faithful pray to you while you may be found; surely the rising of the mighty waters will not reach them. You are my hiding place; you will protect me from trouble and surround me with songs of deliverance"* *(Psalm 32:1–7).*

In Psalm 32, sin is described as a type of decay. Note that "my bones wasted away." It is also described as "heavy," a burden. It is one that we shouldn't have to carry. In Him, we gain all the strength we need to be encouraged.

> *"Blessed is the one whose transgressions are forgiven, whose sins are covered. Blessed is the one whose sin the LORD does not count against them and in whose*

*spirit is no deceit. When I kept silent, my bones wasted
away through my groaning all day long. For day and
night your hand was heavy on me; my strength was
sapped as in the heat of summer. Then I acknowl-
edged my sin to you and did not cover up my iniquity.
I said, "I will confess my transgressions to the Lord."*

Even though we've admitted our sin, we still live in a sinful world.
We will continue to have a need to get rid of sin. Again, the
Word reveals how. Daily help can be found in 1 John 1:9. It's
the Christian's bar of soap. We surrender to Him the thoughts,
actions, words—and the motivations behind them—in which
we've struggled. He forgives us, and then He begins the process
of transforming our minds and changing us so we won't go back
there again. And once we've cleared the air between the Lord and
ourselves, we can clear things up with those around us.

FORGIVE

Interestingly, the Lord used my three sons to help me hone my
forgiveness abilities. They also cured me of being too uptight
about possessions, especially home furnishings.

When the boys were small, I began discovering cracked lamps
from time to time. I got pretty good at putting up a fuss. But
I soon realized that a sweet little child is more precious than any
home accessory. I also realized that one day I will miss the action
in my home. I will miss the little fingerprint smudges on the wall.

Don't get me wrong. I don't want my children to be bulls in china shops. But people are more important than pottery. I decided early on not to invest in any more of the fancy, expensive lamps. The plain ones that got the job done suited me just fine—the cheaper the better.

I carried that new attitude into my refrigerator fiasco. Recently my family and I were talking about how the movers took such care when they were clearing the way for the floor to be repaired. I said, "There's only one thing I really care about." My youngest son Garrett, who is 13 years old, responded, "What's that?" I replied, "You guys. If something gets broken, I won't really be upset. It's just stuff. It's not my treasure."

Then Garrett reminded me of the time he and his big brother were roughhousing. They knocked a beautiful candlestick to the floor, and it cracked in half. He said they were worried about my reaction. But then he smiled and said, "Mom, you came home and calmly said, 'Oh well, I guess we can glue it.' We all looked at each other, expecting you to be upset, and you weren't."

I can say with certainty that Jesus has forgiven me of greater transgressions than a broken candlestick, so I guess I can forgive my boys for being boys. After all, what's most important in life: remaining upset over something that's broken in your life or forgiving others as Christ forgave you?

I hope that you experience the blessing of a loving, forgiving heart—one that's even *generous* in forgiving transgressions. It is a great feeling to truly forgive someone whom you know doesn't deserve it. And the only way we can do that is by applying what His Word says to our minds and actions.

We, as sinners, don't deserve the Lord's grace. But He gives it freely if we just ask Him for it, because He promised to do so in His Word. It is not something we earn—it's free! It is a choice (see Ephesians 2:8–9). Each day we can choose what is better: accepting the mercy of God, or being at the mercy of life.

In addition, forgiving others is a way to unload the guilt and burden of our own sin. "For if you forgive other people when they sin against you, your heavenly Father will also forgive you. But if you do not forgive others their sins, your Father will not forgive your sins" (Matthew 6:14–15). Also note, "Therefore let all the faithful pray to you while you may be found" (Psalm 32:6). This reminds us that we don't have eternity to decide if we will be faithful. Our time is short here on earth. We should choose God. We don't know what will happen tomorrow or exactly how long we have to live.

OBEY HIS WORD

We need to make sure we stay on the path the Lord wants us to. And God's Word is the guide we need to follow. We follow our doctors' orders, don't we—or at least we should.

I found that knowledge from my doctors and the latest research were empowering. I felt better knowing more about the disease I was doing battle with. The more information the better. I wanted to empower others as well. And the knowledge of God's Word was the best part. I knew God had a plan for me, and I was going to abide by that plan wherever it led me. "Hold on to instruction, do not let it go; guard it well, for it is your life" (Proverbs 4:13).

There isn't anything more basic to follow to keep us on the right track than the Ten Commandments. Here is a shortened, personal version of the originals in Deuteronomy 5:6–21:

1. God is number one in my life.

2. I will worship Him, not any other idol.

3. I will praise and bless God's name—and never dishonor Him.

4. I will remember to rest in His holy presence as He has commanded in His Word.

5. I will honor my father and mother.

6. I will not murder another human being.

7. I will not commit adultery.

8. I will not steal.

9. I will not give false witness against anyone.

10. I will not covet my neighbor's house.

Sometimes we can slip into sin and not even realize it by putting other things in our lives (false gods) above God. This isn't one of those tests you can cram for at the last minute. We need to prepare before the winds blow, the rains shift, and the leaks come. Hide Scripture in your heart so you can benefit. If you are facing surgery like I did, you can't take your eyeglasses into surgery. Memorize! What Scripture do you have memorized to recall in case of an emergency? (There will be an emergency!) The Holy Spirit can give you the Word, but we are told in the Bible to *hide* it in our hearts. "Accept instruction from his mouth and lay up his words in your heart" (Job 22:22).

To honor the Word, I'm going to let the Word's own words speak in the following passages. Let the Lord speak to you as you ponder them.

> *"The Lord commanded us to obey all these decrees and to fear the LORD our God, so that we might always prosper and be kept alive, as is the case today. And if we are careful to obey all this law before the LORD our God, as he has commanded us, that will be our righteousness"* (Deuteronomy 6:24–25).

> *"The precepts of the Lord are right, giving joy to the heart. The commands of the LORD are radiant, giving light to the eyes. The fear of the LORD is pure, enduring forever. The decrees of the LORD are firm, and all of them are righteous. They are more precious than gold, than much pure gold; they are sweeter than honey, than honey from the honeycomb. By them your servant is warned; in keeping them there is great reward"* (Psalm 19:8–11).

Following God's Word isn't just the key to staying on the straight and narrow; it's also the source of success.

Feel free to recite the prayer of Jabez:

> *"'Let your hand be with me, and keep me from harm so that I will be free from pain.' And God granted his request"* (1 Chronicles 4:10).

Jotham followed that principle in the Old Testament. He "waged war against the king of the Ammonites and conquered them. That year the Ammonites paid him a hundred talents of silver, ten thousand cors of wheat and ten thousand cors of barley. The Ammonites brought him the same amount also in the second and third years. Jotham grew powerful because he walked steadfastly before the LORD his God" (2 Chronicles 27:5–6).

> *"For they [His Words] are life to those who find them and health to one's whole body. Above all else, guard your heart, for everything you do flows from it. Keep your mouth free of perversity; keep corrupt talk far from your lips. Let your eyes look straight ahead; fix your gaze directly before you. Give careful thought to the paths for your feet and be steadfast in all your ways. Do not turn to the right or the left; keep your foot from evil"* (Proverbs 4:22–27).

> *"Surely the righteous will never be shaken; they will be remembered forever"* (Psalm 112:6).

> *"The Redeemer will come to Zion, to those in Jacob who repent of their sins,"* declares the LORD. *"As for me this is my covenant with them,"* says the LORD. *"My Spirit, who is on you, will not depart from you, and my words that I have put in your mouth will always be on your lips, on the lips of your children and on the mouths of their descendants — from this*

time on and forever," says the LORD
(Isaiah 59:20–21).

"If you love me, keep my commands. And I will ask
the Father, and he will give you another advocate
to help you and be with you forever — the Spirit of
truth. The world cannot accept him, because it nei-
ther sees him nor knows him. But you know him, for
he lives with you and will be in you. I will not leave
you as orphans; I will come to you. Before long, the
world will not see me anymore, but you will see me.
Because I live, you also will live" (John 14:15–19).

Referring back to the Lord's Prayer from a previous chapter, we are taught to ask, "And lead us not into temptation." Ask God to help us to not fall into sin. "But deliver us from the evil one"—from every evil, and from the cause of evil, who is the devil. God's Word is our ultimate aid in fighting off both temptation and evil. The Lord's Prayer finishes with the assurance of the fulfillment of our request, for to God belongs an eternal kingdom filled with His power and glory, and we get to share that.

The bottom line: Obey God's instructions and you will be blessed. You will be blessed wherever you go. Not only that, but your children will be blessed as well by your obedience to God.

But wait, there's more good news. You aren't just blessed today or tomorrow, or for this week—you are blessed for eternity. He is the same God through the generations. He never changes.

"Those who are wise will shine like the brightness of the heavens, and those who lead many to righteousness, like the stars for ever and ever" (Daniel 12:3). Are you willing to shine brightly and lead many to righteousness?

HAVE FAITH

Sometimes following God's Word (along with prayer) doesn't produce immediate results. That's where faith can step in and help you in the storm. A few years ago, a lot of storms came our way, including a job situation. I prayed hard about the situation, and I kept getting the numbers 2521 back as an answer.

I heard those digits mentioned on the radio, and then I saw them on a license tag. Finally I heard them talked about again on the radio as a preacher read from Matthew 25:21, and then I understood what the Lord was trying to tell me. It was the parable of the talents: "His master replied, 'Well done, good and faithful servant! You have been faithful with a few things; I will put you in charge of many things. Come and share your master's happiness.'" God increases what we sow!

> *"Again Jesus began to teach by the lake. The crowd that gathered around him was so large that he got into a boat and sat in it out on the lake, while all the people were along the shore at the water's edge. He taught them many things by parables, and in his teaching said: 'Listen! A farmer went out to sow his seed. As he was scattering the seed, some fell*

along the path, and the birds came and ate it up. Some fell on rocky places, where it did not have much soil. It sprang up quickly, because the soil was shallow. But when the sun came up, the plants were scorched, and they withered because they had no root. Other seed fell among thorns, which grew up and choked the plants, so that they did not bear grain. Still other seed fell on good soil. It came up, grew and produced a crop, some multiplying thirty, some sixty, some a hundred times.' Then Jesus said, 'Whoever has ears to hear, let them hear.'

"When he was alone, the Twelve and the others around him asked him about the parables. He told them, 'The secret of the kingdom of God has been given to you. But to those on the outside everything is said in parables so that, 'they may be ever seeing but never perceiving, and ever hearing but never understanding; otherwise they might turn and be forgiven!'"

"Then Jesus said to them, 'Don't you understand this parable? How then will you understand any parable? The farmer sows the word. Some people are like seed along the path, where the word is sown. As soon as they hear it, Satan comes and takes away the word that was sown in them. Others, like seed sown on rocky places, hear the word and at once receive it with joy. But since they have no root, they last only a short time. When trouble or persecution comes because of the word, they quickly fall away.

"'Still others, like seed sown among thorns, hear the word; but the worries of this life, the deceitfulness of wealth and the desires for other things come in and choke the word, making it unfruitful. Others, like seed sown on good soil, hear the word, accept it, and produce a crop — some thirty, some sixty, some a hundred times what was sown.'

"He said to them, 'Do you bring in a lamp to put it under a bowl or a bed? Instead, don't you put it on its stand? For whatever is hidden is meant to be disclosed, and whatever is concealed is meant to be brought out into the open. If anyone has ears to hear, let them hear.'

"'Consider carefully what you hear,' he continued. 'With the measure you use, it will be measured to you — and even more. Whoever has will be given more; whoever does not have, even what they have will be taken from them'" (Mark 4:1–25).

Just reading His Word isn't enough. We need to act on it. And when things don't change right away, we need to just believe that the Lord will make it happen in time.

When Jesus went to spread the good news in His own home town, they were so familiar with Him that they would not open their spirit to the Savior.

"Coming to his hometown, he began teaching the people in their synagogue, and they were amazed.

'Where did this man get this wisdom and these
miraculous powers?' they asked. 'Isn't this the car-
penter's son? Isn't his mother's name Mary, and
aren't his brothers James, Joseph, Simon and Judas?

"Aren't all his sisters with us? Where then did
this man get all these things?' And they took offense
at him.

"But Jesus said to them, 'A prophet is not without
honor except in his own town and in his own home.'
And he did not do many miracles there because of
their lack of faith" (Matthew 13:54–58).

We can gain more insight about the same incident in Mark's Gospel as well: "He could not do any miracles there, except lay his
hands on a few sick people and heal them. He was amazed at their
lack of faith" (6:5–6).

Faith that God will keep His Word has power. It is transforming
power. I had faith God would carry me through cancer. I didn't
know if I would be healed here or in heaven, but it was a relief to
know that God had my back. He told me so in His Word.

TRUST

Practicing your faith will lead to an unshakable trust in your heart.
As God delivers you from storm after storm, your trust in Him
becomes a habit.

During my first cancer treatment, I had a close encounter with
disaster. Thank God that my husband had accompanied me. He

was preparing to do play-by-play for a college football game, so he studied his prep work as we sat there.

The oncology nurse began the infusion. I sat there and prayed that the chemo would destroy any cancer cells floating around in my body. As the chemo entered the vein in my arm, I felt a strange sensation of heat start at the bottom of my belly and work its way up to my heart.

As it reached my heart, I could feel my heart being suppressed and slowing down. I could barely speak and call out for help. It turns out I was allergic to the chemo. The nurse came over and stopped the procedure. Then she gave me some Benadryl, we started up again. I was just fine this time, but it was a little scary. I had to trust God. He pulled me through what was a horrifying situation.

Strangely, my second bout with cancer was harder for me than the first. I really hadn't questioned God back then. I think I needed Him too much to question Him. I just reached up for my Father's hand and let Him carry me through the storm. I certainly did not want cancer. But through cancer, He molded me, showed me blessings, and more. I admit I was in shock, but I clung to the Lord and let Him lead me.

"But we have this treasure in jars of clay to show that this all-surpassing power is from God and not from us. We are hard pressed on every side, but not crushed; perplexed, but not in despair; persecuted, but not abandoned; struck down, but not destroyed. Therefore we do not lose heart. Though outwardly we are wasting away, yet inwardly we are being renewed day by

day. For our light and momentary troubles are achieving for us an eternal glory that far outweighs them all. So we fix our eyes not on what is seen, but on what is unseen, since what is seen is temporary, but what is unseen is eternal" (2 Corinthians 4:7–9, 16–18).

GOD'S TREADMILL

As a part of a new attitude I am adopting, I believe God provides what is good in life to help keep us healthy and happy. Recently I had fallen off the exercise wagon. I allowed myself to try to eat away stress and frustration. But guess what? Gaining weight and devouring sugary treats only made me feel worse, and more frustrated about my condition.

So I signed up my family for a health club program. It wasn't just for me; the rest of the family loved it too. The guys enjoy playing basketball almost every day if time allows. For the first time in a long time, I jumped into an exercise class. Wow, was I in over my head. This was far different than the dance exercise classes I had taken for years. This had weights and big balls and positions that were very foreign to my body.

I was blessed to have a friend from my kids' school right next to me, guiding me through. God was good to provide me with this angel. While we were hopping, lugging, and lifting, I was silently praying. *Lord, help me not to break something or to have my heart pop right here in this class.*

Oh how I wished I had prepared more for this reentry into exercise class! I recalled how my friend and I had both trained for marathons. I had even trained a short time after surgery and during chemo. I figured that this class would be no problem. If I had only walked on the treadmill a little longer! I thought, *Oh no, I may not make it until the end.*

Everyone else in class was skinny and in shape—the way I used to be. I had told my son logically, "If I just follow around the skinny ladies and do everything they do and eat everything they do, I will be skinny in no time." So I hung in there, too embarrassed to leave. My friend stayed beside me, smiling and encouraging me until my "torture" ended.

The whole experience reminded me about how important it is to be prepared *spiritually and physically.* By training physically, I can be ready for anything. By reading my Bible and praying to stay connected to God's will, I can also be ready for anything in life. When that storm or comment comes flying at us and catches us off guard, we won't have to stop and think, *How can I deal with this?* We will already know we can rely on the Holy Spirit to remind us through God's comforting and powerful Word.

(While we are on the subject of exercise, after you read this, get up and walk, jump, or dance.) Moving is a gift from God. He designed our bodies to be used. It will make you feel great. There are also studies that show that exercise reduces your risk of cancer. Exercise has also been found to lengthen our lives.

I felt that floundering through to the end of my exercise class was a monumental achievement, but finishing well in life should be our main focus. That reminds me of an incident recently when our family had gone to the movies.

The most amazing thing I saw was not on the silver screen. The most inspiring thing was right in front of us in line: a young man with no hands and no legs, sitting in a wheelchair. Yet he got his credit card out of his wallet with his arms, and bought his ticket.

As he made his way to the door, I said, "Let me get that for you." He cheerfully replied, "I got it." He proceeded to pop open the door and roll himself in. I looked at our boys and said, "We should never complain about anything again!"

Even more encouraging is what happened when I put that story on Facebook. It received almost 600 positive responses. Don't underestimate yourself! With God, all things are possible! That man's ease in maneuvering a night out at the movies showed me that *we* are the ones who limit ourselves.

When you persevere and keep going even when it's tough, even when it hurts, that's when you grow. Not only in your muscles, but also in your faith. Keep trusting. Keep holding onto the Lord for His encouragement and direction. Just like when running a marathon, you have to keep putting one foot in front of the other during tough times. I have run five marathons and five half-marathons. As my marathon coach would yell as we prepared to go up a hill, "Pick 'em up and put 'em down!" In other words, "Keep going!" Push through the pain and fatigue. Dig deep into God's Word and His love so you can stay strong in the storms.

I wrote down and memorized Bible verses to help me keep going in my marathon running. I would even say them out loud, or tell them to the runner next to me. "I can do all things through Christ who strengthens me!" That's how God works: your own encouragement is encouragement for others. Your faith can be living and breathing. God's Word can flow through you to bless you and bless others.

While I was praying for strength out loud and reciting Bible verses at about mile 20, a man I never saw was behind me listening. I finished the race, not in record time, but in God's time. Weeks later, I received a sweet email from a man who thanked me for the encouragement. He said those Bible verses kept him going too! It's like the sap in a vine; it flows through many branches.

When I was in college, I found myself stretched and challenged. There were times I wondered if I could make it. God put encouragers in my life. My mom was one of the greatest encouragers, reminding me that I could do it. My big sister in my sorority would help encourage me. She gave me a poster with a poem on it called "Don't Quit":

When things go wrong, as they sometimes will,
When the road you're trudging seems all uphill,
When the funds are low and the debts are high,
And you want to smile, but you have to sigh,
When care is pressing you down a bit,
Rest, if you must, but don't you quit.

Life is queer with its twists and turns,
As every one of us sometimes learns,
And many a failure turns about,
When he might have won had he stuck it out;
Don't give up though the pace seems slow–
You may succeed with another blow.

Often the goal is nearer than
It seems to a faint and faltering man,
Often the struggler has given up,
When he might have captured the victor's cup,
And he learned too late when the night slipped down,
How close he was to the golden crown.

Success is failure turned inside out–
The silver tint of the clouds of doubt,
And you never can tell how close you are,
It may be near when it seems so far,
So stick to the fight when you're hardest hit–
It's when things seem worst that you mustn't quit.

Don't give in to discouragement. Keep the faith. God has something better in store for you. "Do not let your hearts be troubled. You believe in God; believe also in me" (John 14:1).

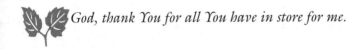 *God, thank You for all You have in store for me.*

Our Key Scripture

"We proclaim to you what we have seen and heard, so that you also may have fellowship with us. And our fellowship is with the Father and with his Son, Jesus Christ" (1 JOHN 1:3).

Fellowship in the Storm

*O*ur heavenly Father, Jesus, the Holy Spirit, and His love toward us through our family and friends are all vital to us during the storms in our lives. How would we otherwise get through the good, bad, and even the ugly?

Maybe help from someone else is as nearby as your spouse. Mine was there for me for every wave that crashed against me during my cancer storm.

The reason that I had to do chemo at all was because a couple of pathologists had found some microscopic disease in two of my lymph nodes. When I met my oncologist Dr. Cantrell for the first time, I felt like a deer in headlights. I knew I should be more scared that my cancer might return, but for some reason I was even more scared of the chemo than I had been of the surgery. I couldn't comprehend much of what he was saying, except that if I did the chemo, I'd have a good chance of never seeing a recurrence. This was, in fact, our battle plan.

But was the *fear* of the chemo worse than actually going through it? I shared that fear with my broadcast viewers as

I walked them through the next phase in my fight. On the set that night, I read:

> Seven weeks ago, I had surgery for breast cancer, and I shared that with you to remind you to keep a check on your own health. Now that battle continues, and as we promised, we'll continue to walk you through the process. For the next few weeks, I'll tell you about my fight to show you how life goes on. Before I began chemotherapy, I wondered if the dread of it was worse than the actual experience. So far that's turned out to be true. I feared the worst, but learned I could make it.

The director then rolled the story.

Breast cancer. First came the diagnosis.

DOUG BELL [MY HUSBAND]: *It was like somebody punched me in the solar plexus.*

BRENDA [ME]: *I remember trembling as I listened to the surgeon after the biopsy. She said it was cancer. Our spring break vacation to Disney was off, and a mastectomy had to be scheduled.*

DOUG: *I was shocked, but then I looked at you. You had that look of determination like you wanted to tackle it, so it made me feel a lot better.*

BRENDA: *Together we fielded one of life's curve balls. And it felt like I was on a rollercoaster, trying to gather information and make all the right decisions. A little more than a week after the diagnosis, I was in surgery for a mastectomy.*

DOUG: *After the initial surgery, Dr. Winchester came in and said that the cancer was more widespread than first thought.*

BRENDA: *The doctor decided I'd have a better chance of beating the cancer with a double mastectomy, and my husband agreed.*

DOUG: *The chances of the same thing happening in the other breast were pretty good. I knew it was the best thing for you. It was really the only decision.*

BRENDA: *But even with the double mastectomy, I still had about a 50 percent chance that the cancer would appear somewhere else in my body, because it had spread to my lymph nodes. That's why the next step in the fight had to be chemotherapy.*

This is one of the baddest of the bad boys in the chemo line—Adriamycin. Some people call this one the red devil. Hopefully it will seek out and kill any cancer cells floating around the body. The allied forces of chemo drugs Adriamycin and Cytoxan and Taxol will give me more than a fighting chance. The worst part of the treatment is a prick in the arm from the initial needle. The battle is on, because once the breast cancer cells attach to another organ and form a tumor, it's a whole different ball game.

The plan of attack includes 1) Adriamycin, which comes from a fungus, 2) Cytoxan, which was developed from a chemical warfare substance (it's a cousin to mustard gas), and 3) Taxol, which comes from the leaves of a yew tree.

Remember, without the treatment, I'll have about a 50 percent chance of a recurrence. But with this treatment and a five-year cancer prevention drug, my chance of seeing a recurrence is 8 percent or less. That's a chance I can live with, even if it means I'll lose my hair because of the chemo drugs.

DR. CANTRELL: *That will be lethal for the cancer cell and not for the patient, although it may be lethal for some of your other cells, like your hair follicles. But it is not permanently lethal for your hair. With Adriamycin, you will definitely lose your hair.*

[Video of Brenda trying on wig]

But that's why they make wigs. You can buy hair, and it's only temporary. The other symptoms are nausea and fatigue.

[Brenda at home holding medicine bottles]

I take this medication for nausea. This is a steroid for energy, and it helps prevent infections. Then every now and then, I have to take a rest and say, "See ya, guys."

[Video of cheese crackers]

But even with the antinausea medication, when that sick feeling creeps in during the day, cheese crackers help fend it off.

[Chemotherapy video]

The other thing the doctor must watch closely is the white blood cell count. Those white cells fend off disease, but chemotherapy lowers those counts and leaves the patient open to infections.

[Video of Brenda at work on the phone]

This week I passed my test. The white count is just high enough so that I will be allowed to continue working [video of me playing with children] and playing. The rule is that I must rest when I feel I need it. My new regimen includes more naps, less stress, and enjoying every moment as it comes. And, of course, more prayer.

Doug: *Brenda's one of the strongest people I know—small in stature, but strong. Does that come from faith? I think so!*

[Brenda on set]

My family, faith, and friends continue to give me strength. A special thanks to my husband, Doug, for being my knight in shining armor throughout this fight. By the way, the dread of chemo *was* worse than the actual treatment.

What I should have included in that report was the fact that I really appreciated my husband's company at the treatments. One day, they even set us up in an open room, with a bed and a chair for Doug. On that day, we were granted the opportunity to be together, almost alone in the room, with the exception of the chemo nurse who would come in and administer the drugs and chemo into my veins. For those couple of hours, he sat with me, and we got a chance to talk, joke, and just be together. That was the upside of having chemo that day: getting to spend some quality time with my husband.

As Doug and I were leaving, he told me he'd been reading an old copy of "People Magazine" that featured famous breast-cancer survivors. He said, "I didn't know Olivia Newton-John had breast cancer." I said, "I didn't realize that either." He went on to say that Peggy Fleming also had it, and he mentioned several other famous women too. Just knowing that those strong, beautiful women had it, dealt with it, and survived, was a comfort.

FELLOWSHIP FEEDS PERSEVERANCE

Doug is not the only person I received encouragement from. I'd heard that for some people, eating lunch right after treatment helped. For me it seemed to. A nice salad and a hot bowl of French onion soup seemed to soothe me. I'd come home and lay down for 30 minutes or an hour before getting up and going to work. I just wanted life to be normal.

Going to work was normal. I didn't want to let anyone down. That's why I kept trudging along. There were many days I felt like I was in a fog. I was tired beyond belief. I remember the fatigue after the first chemo treatment. I came home to have dinner with Doug and the children and, after eating a few bites, I said, "I'm just going to lay down for 10 minutes." Thirty-five minutes later, Doug rustled me from what felt like a deep sleep.

"Are you going to go back to work?" he asked.

I jumped up like a school kid who had just heard the school bus honking in front of the house. My heart pounded and I felt like I was moving in slow motion while I tried to shake off the fatigue. I kissed everyone good-bye and hopped in the car to go back to work. The nausea hit me at the red light just before I got on the highway. I had the medicine Dr. Cantrell had given me. As I neared the TV station 10 minutes away, the nausea was rising to a crescendo.

I made it to my desk and called the nurse on call. I wanted to be sure it was OK to take this medicine and drive back home. I'm glad I checked.

Dr. Cantrell called me back to ask how I was doing. I said, "Dr. Cantrell, I think I might need that stronger antinausea medicine you prescribed. But I just wanted to know if it would be OK to take it before the news."

He said with a chuckle, "If you take that medicine, you may not make it to do the news. And if you do, you might be singing the news."

"OK," I said. "That answers my question. Since I have to drive home later, I guess I'll try to hold off."

I hung up and thought, *Oh no, this is getting worse, not better!* Then I thought of the cheese cracker method of nausea control I had heard about from a teacher and neighbor who had breast cancer a year before me.

I reached into the cabinet above my desk and grabbed the cheese crackers. It was worth a try, because it was 8:35 P.M. I didn't have much time to decide whether or not I could go on.

It was getting so bad. Soon I knew I'd be in the bathroom sick to my stomach. I chomped on one cracker. It didn't help. Then I tried another, and I thought there was a bit of leveling off of the nausea. So I ate a third cracker. It was better! It wasn't perfect, but I knew I wouldn't horrify the viewing audience by getting sick all over the desk. (Thank you, Helen Dickinson, for saving us all from an embarrassing moment.)

I did push the envelope during chemo. I took walks to keep my strength. Many of those beautiful spring days I was accompanied by our nanny, Nessa, and baby Garrett. I couldn't lift Garrett yet, so Nessa came along to help. I enjoyed our walks and talks. Her stories took my mind off of cancer. It was refreshing. Another cancer patient agreed with me that the walking helped keep the energy level up.

Even my 14-year-old son at the time could see that others can be an encouragement. He had come with me when for a speaking engagement at a church. I enjoyed the fact that he could see what the family of God—the fellowship—looks likes beyond our own individual home church. After the service we went to the fellowship hall, and it seemed there were miles and miles of casseroles, meatballs, and desserts. Garrett lapped up the variety of good-old home cooking.

On the way home he commented that those people were "really, really, nice!" He said, "Mom, that pastor said, 'If you all need anything, and I mean *anything,* you call me.'" "Mom," he said, "I think he really meant it!"

"Garrett, I know he did! That's what I was talking about, being in the family of God. We are truly in a loving family. You should be able to go to *any* church and feel what you felt today—if it's a living, breathing church! You can also experience the kingdom of God here on earth by fellowshipping with believers! You could feel the light there, couldn't you?"

"Yes, Mom!"

FELLOWSHIP WITH JESUS

Yes, as they say in the news business, I buried the lead; I saved some of the best till last. When you feel like your world is crumbling down around you, read Psalm 91.

> *"He will cover you with his feathers. He will shelter you with his wings. His faithful promises are your armor and protection* (v. 4 NLT).
>
> *"Do not be afraid of the terrors of the night, nor the arrow that flies in the day* (v. 5).
>
> *"Do not dread the disease that stalks in darkness, nor the disaster that strikes at midday* (v. 6).
>
> *"Though a thousand fall at your side, though ten thousand are dying around you, these evils will not touch you* (v. 7).
>
> *"If you make the LORD your refuge, if you make the Most High your shelter, no evil will conquer you; no plague will come near your home"* (vv. 9–10).
>
> *"For he will order his angels to protect you wherever you go* (v. 11).

"They will hold you up with their hands so you won't even hurt your foot on a stone (v. 12).

"You will trample upon lions and cobras; you will crush fierce lions and serpents under your feet!" (v. 13).

"The LORD *says, 'I will rescue those who love me. I will protect those who trust in my name'"* (v. 14).

Totally focus on Jesus during and after a storm.

"I love you, LORD, *my strength. The* LORD *is my rock, my fortress and my deliverer; my God is my rock, in whom I take refuge, my shield and the horn of my salvation, my stronghold"* (Psalm 18:1–2).

Can you totally focus on Jesus in the chaos of your day? He can set you free from your burdens.

"As for God, his way is perfect: The LORD's *word is flawless; he shields all who take refuge in him. For who is God besides the* LORD? *And who is the Rock except our God? It is God who arms me with strength and keeps my way secure. He makes my feet like the feet of a deer; he causes me to stand on the heights. He trains my hands for battle; my arms can bend a bow of bronze. You make your saving help my shield; your help has made me great. You*

armed me with strength for battle; you humbled my adversaries before me" (2 Samuel 22:31–36, 40).

In Philippians 3, Paul says he considers everything a loss compared to the greatness of knowing the Lord. Your job, income, home, and possessions are nothing compared to knowing the Lord. This is great news in so many ways. In fact, it should be a huge relief. It reconfirms what Jesus told Martha: that Mary was choosing something better. Focusing on the Lord and not fretting over the tasks at hand should release us from stress. No matter what we have on our plates we know that the Lord is much more important and wonderful!

There are many voices in this world telling us what to do, how to think, how to act. We must not accept confusion. Totally focus on Christ. Here is the great news: there is no condemnation when we are in Christ!

> *"The LORD is close to the brokenhearted and saves those who are crushed in spirit. The righteous person may have many troubles, but the LORD delivers him from them all; he protects all his bones, not one of them will be broken. Evil will slay the wicked; the foes of the righteous will be condemned. The LORD will rescue his servants; no one who takes refuge in him will be condemned"* (Psalm 34:18–22).

"But the LORD will not leave them in the power of the wicked or let them be condemned when brought to trial" (Psalm 37:33).

By the law of God, you are set free from the law of sin and death. But in order to be free, you must focus totally on Christ. Here is a Scripture you can repeat to yourself in times of need. Use it to help you totally focus on the Lord.

> "Jesus replied, 'Love the LORD your God with all your heart and with all your soul and with all your mind.' This is the first and greatest commandment. And the second is like it: 'Love your neighbor as yourself.' All the Law and the Prophets hang on these two commandments" (Matthew 22:37–40).

May all of these words help you find refreshment, hope, and courage in the Lord Jesus Christ.

Our Key Scriptures

"Come to me, all you who are weary and burdened, and I will give you rest. Take my yoke upon you and learn from me, for I am gentle and humble in heart, and you will find rest for your souls. For my yoke is easy and my burden is light"
(Matthew 11:28–30).

"But one thing I do: Forgetting what is behind and straining toward what is ahead, I press on toward the goal to win the prize for which God has called me heavenward in Christ Jesus" (Philippians 3:13–14).

CHAPTER 8

When You Think You Can't Go On

LEARNING TO "CHILL"

My husband is away so many weekends when he is covering golf or football. The boys and I hunker down in front of the college football games together. It had become tradition for my youngest son's neighbor friends to join us for tailgate food. It's usually chicken wings, chicken fingers, and pizza. Oh, and I would never forget the cookies.

As I have watched my own boys grow into young men, I have also watched these two friends. On this particular Saturday we were all talking and observed that all of the boys' ages ranged from 13 to 15. I told them I had enjoyed watching them grow up, and I reminded them our home is their home any time.

While they started the football party downstairs, I was under orders to tidy up our playroom upstairs. Another friend, who just happened to be a girl, might be coming over.

As a boy-mom, I have learned that cleaning up for a bunch of guys is much different than cleaning for one special girl. That kind of clean must include nooks and crannies. It must also include a spotless bathroom with the seat left down.

So I dug in and scooped out as much boy-dirt as possible. The guinea pig Miss Piggy watched with great curiosity. I vacuumed, sprayed, and polished. Finally it was done! It was a cleaning masterpiece. No applause, please.

About that time the boys downstairs were talking about playing Ping-Pong upstairs. They discussed whether it was worth entering the clean zone, because, as I had made perfectly clear, "Whatever you mess up, you must clean up." Finally one of the brave boys ventured up and into the room. After he crossed the threshold of the room, he backed out in a stunned voice: "Whoa! I can't go in there. It's too clean!"

I laughed so hard. I asked, "You mean the room is so clean that it's making you uncomfortable!? There is definitely something wrong with that." He did go in, and he did clean up his cups and drinks. And, after all that sweat, the young lady couldn't come over after all. But at least we had an amazingly clean room!

This may sound funny, but as a homeroom mom, I would stay up late trying to create a delicious treat that would make the kids say, *Oh wow!* One year I made little peanut-butter sandwiches that I cut into the shape of a Christmas tree for the third-grade Christmas party. Not only did I cut them into Christmas trees, I sprayed them green with frosting spray. But that wasn't enough, so I decorated the little sandwich trees with red frosting balls.

I was so tired the next morning, and I had made a terrible mess in the kitchen, but we were going to have the cutest treat ever! (Pride.) Then, you know what happened? I was humbled. The kids barely looked at the tree sandwiches! Almost no one even took a bite!

My heart sank. I just wanted someone to appreciate the hours I put into these little works of art that would soon be heading to the classroom trash can untouched by the children's hands. Perhaps they equated green with vegetables? No matter. Whatever the reason for the snack rejection, it had happened.

I learned a lesson. Keep it simple. I shouldn't get so caught up in trying to make something so perfect that I lose sight of the party itself. That's what was important—just letting the kids have a little fun. It didn't really matter what was on their plates. "When pride comes, then comes disgrace, but with humility comes wisdom" (Proverbs 11:2).

You would think I had learned my lesson, right? As the room mom one year, I told the teacher I would make Lady Bug cupcakes. She even printed the directions for me. It wasn't just a one- or two-step process. These lady bug cupcakes kept me up until three in the morning. I had to get the frosting red. Red! Do you know how much red food coloring it takes to turn white frosting into red and not just pink?

I had to get the right kind of Dove Bar candy for the little head, and some sort of licorice to line the wings! I was determined to get it right! And I did. But I got no sleep that night. I won the contest! But did I? My pride to be a Supermom caused me to spend hours on cupcakes that the children barely noticed before they devoured.

Have you ever prepared for a guest, but by the time the guest arrived you were almost too exhausted to truly enjoy the visit? As a hostess, I hope I have matured and become seasoned, efficient, and more relaxed. These are key ingredients in the recipe for good hospitality.

In fact, the best compliment I guess I could have gotten from my college kid was, "Hey, yeah, Mom. You are more chill!" Becoming *more chill* is a big deal for a recovering type-A personality. For me it comes from having confidence in the Lord that He will take care of every situation.

The bar seems to rise every year our children gain. First, there is park baseball. Then there is a higher level called travel ball. Then there are the elite teams. It just goes on and on. Competition in youth sports alone is tougher and tougher every year.

I don't remember kids in my neighborhood who had personal trainers when I was growing up, but today that is not unusual. Academics are also more competitive these days. There is one school that has a 400 percent increase in students who are taking college prep classes. Yes, that's 400 percent!

I now have a son in college, and everyone agrees that just getting into a college, much less competing for scholarships, is more competitive. Now don't get me wrong. Competition can be good. As it is written in Proverbs, "As iron sharpens iron, so friend sharpens a friend" (27:17 NLT).

When competition is healthy, it is good. But just like anything on this earth, too much of anything can be bad. It can become an addiction. Are you racing to be the best _____ (fill in the blank)? Is that fight to be the best _____ separating you from your true mission of glorifying God? Is there an area of your life that keeps you spinning your wheels to measure up? Try become a little *more chill.* I guess it's all about patience.

SURRENDER THE FISH ALREADY

Somehow as a parent I get convinced to say yes to things, when I should probably say no. Remember when my child wanted fish (not for dinner but in a tank), so we had fish? Well, the story went on.

As with any pet situation, the children's promises to take care of "it" later end up with mom as the caretaker. I like dogs and don't mind any cleanup or feeding duties there, but fish are not my cup of tea. However, for my children I would do just about anything. So that's why we had fish.

Of course, when the kids were busy at school and with sports, I often relented and cleaned the fish tank. Scraping scum off the glass walls was something I'd never dreamed I'd be doing. I became fond of the little creatures. I actually liked the angel fish. But just before we went on a family vacation to South Florida, one of the two angels checked out, passed on, left us. So then there was just the one!

I had asked our sweet neighbor Dianne to throw a little fish food in the tank while we were gone. It was a great vacation — busy and tiring. By the time it ended, I needed a vacation from the vacation. At the time, we had two dogs, two small children, and a fish, not to mention full-time jobs. With all of that going on,

I remember dreading the condition of the fish tank as we were pulling back into the driveway.

I managed a small prayer, but apparently a powerful one. I said, "Lord, with dogs and babies and work, I don't think I can handle a fish too. Lord, anytime you take that fish away is OK by me."

As we arrived at our front door, sweet Dianne thrust her body between the front door and us. She asked to talk to me in the playroom, where the fish tank sat.

She said, "Brenda, I have bad news. Your fish died. I am so sorry!" She continued, "I was gonna go get you another one, but you got home sooner than I had expected."

"No! Please don't get another one."

Then she said, "I saved him for you. He is in my freezer wrapped in aluminum foil. I saved him so you could have a service for him."

After the demise of our last angel, I tried to surrender how I committed my time to God. That includes trying not to do it all by having every kind of pet under the sun. Yes, often what we think is the destination is really just the start of a journey.

I always chuckle at the show *The Bachelor* or *The Bachelorette*. I think they should just throw the young prospects into a house together with a leaky roof, a throwing-up baby, a dog that just ate the couch, and three other young children who need rides to football practice, dance lessons, and the tutor all at the same time. The guy who handles that with grace and humor should get the girl!

Did your dreams get derailed? It's OK to let God know how you feel. Let Him know. But don't stay mad at God. People die, steal, cheat, and let us down. But the good news is that God is our Rock. He is always there and never changes.

How can you get past the hurt and allow God to heal you? By truly letting go and moving on. "Refrain from anger and turn from wrath; do not fret—it leads only to evil" (Psalm 37:8).

Recognize evil. Sin can be born from bitterness and anger. Trust God to take what seems like an impossible, heartbreaking situation and produce healing and something good from it.

Allow the Lord to bless you. Accept His goodness in your life.

Our Key Scripture

"Give all your worries and cares to God, for he cares about you" (1 PETER 5:7 NLT).

Racing into His Arms

GOING PUBLIC

In January 2001, the year was starting out pretty well—so well in fact that I prayed to God about it. "Lord, why am I so blessed? I have a great husband, great kids, a great home, and a wonderful job. I feel like I'm not doing enough to deserve all this. Why me, Lord? Why did you choose me to have such a great life, when so many others are suffering?"

A few weeks later I was enjoying a hot bubble bath and a good book. This ritual was my way of unwinding. (I was usually so busy that I had to put "relaxing" on my list of things to do, just so I'd fit it in!) This was a rare, quiet, peaceful moment, and I savored it. While I soaked in the warm water, I thought my breasts felt a little funny, but I figured it must be because my period was coming on.

I also remembered that, while I was driving home earlier in the week, I had a familiar feeling in my right breast—as though it had filled up with milk. It was the same feeling I'd had while I was expecting my children. I remember thinking, *I can't be pregnant!*

As I lathered up, I noticed a pea-sized lump in my right breast. To the right of that was an egg-shaped mass. I'd always had lumpy, bumpy breasts. But there was something different about these two places. Trying to blow it off as probably nothing, I jumped into some flannel pajamas and turned on the TV. An *Oprah* rerun was airing.

It was then that I remembered her show from a few nights before. The guest was a woman who had battled breast cancer while living at the South Pole. She had mentioned a deadly type of breast cancer that first showed up as an egg-shaped mass, which then grew cancer cells that traveled to the brain.

I began to worry. I got a cold chill, even with my warm flannels on. I told myself, *I'm overreacting. I should probably get my yearly checkup soon anyway.*

Being a busy working Mom, I put off calling the doctor for a few weeks. I told my husband about the lump, and of course he urged me to go check it out. I had wanted him to say it was probably nothing.

I found ways to be too busy to rush to the doctor's office. I like to think of myself as an intelligent person, but delaying this doctor visit was not the brightest thing I've ever done. Two weeks after I discovered the lump, I mentioned to Doug again that it was still there. He said, "Call Dr. Snowden today. It's probably nothing, but just get it checked out."

I'll never forget the day when, less than two hours from news time, I got a call at my desk from a lab tech. She said, "We have your results. I can't tell you anything except your doctor will take good care of you. Your doctor just got the results this afternoon and will probably contact you very soon."

I felt like someone had just poured cold water through my veins. This didn't sound good. But again I assured myself this was nothing to worry about. I hung up the phone, and literally a few seconds later the phone rang again. The doctor. My journey through cancer had begun. But this was only one part of it.

The next project was to write and tape my announcement for the day of surgery. Imagine trying to come up with a script telling the world you have breast cancer. I consulted with Liz Hurley, a news anchor in Huntsville, Alabama, who had also had breast cancer. She even lost her mother to the disease as a child. She urged me to be honest, real, and "tell it like it is." I sat at my desk, tapped away at the keyboard, and wrote the most important message of my life. This announcement aired on the 6:00 news while I was still in surgery.

"My husband saved my life, and here's how. About a month ago I felt a lump in my breast and, at the urging of my husband, I had a mammogram. While the lump I found turned out to be nothing to worry about, the doctor found an early form of breast cancer. She had a previous mammogram to compare it to, one that I had right here at ABC 33/40 less than a year before. It clearly showed there were major breast changes. That led to a biopsy and diagnosis that I did in fact have breast cancer. My doctor believes we caught the cancer early, and with surgery, doctors say the odds are in my favor. I have a very good chance of getting rid of it.

"Right now I am either still in surgery or have just gotten out of it. I plan to meet this latest challenge in my life head on and fight. And fight for your health as well by urging women to do breast self-exams and to get mammograms, and for men to get cancer screenings. This silent disease struck me, and I had no clue it was invading my body. Right now, I feel just fine. That's why regular checks for cancer are so important.

"Remember, early detection is the key. If my sharing my diagnosis saves one life, then it will be worth everything I'm going through. Together we can do battle with a killer and win. And with the help of my doctors, family, friends, and faith, it will be OK.

"Fighting for you, Brenda Ladun ABC 33/40."

Then my co-anchor Josh Thomas made the announcement that, instead of sending flowers, well-wishers could make donations to the Susan G. Komen Breast Cancer Foundation. He also went on to announce the fact that ABC 33/40 was providing free mammograms in my honor through a local hospital. The next Saturday, more than a hundred women got free mammograms at St. Vincent's Mammography Center, located at a local shopping center.

I didn't know how people would react to the announcement of my cancer diagnosis and treatment. I guess I didn't think about it. There had been no time that week to think about anything except getting myself and my family prepared for the surgery.

THE SURGERY

The morning of surgery, I kept thinking about several Bible verses. Proverbs 3:5 rolled around in my head: "Trust in the LORD with all your heart, do not depend on your own understanding" (NLT).

At 5:30 in the morning on February 26, 2001, I was mentally preparing to go into surgery. I gave Doug my miracle medal that my friend Lisa Baggett gave me. It is a Catholic medal that represents hope. Even though we're Baptists and don't know much about Catholic medals, it made me feel better to know that my friend and her church were praying for us. Doug held it for me—he put it on that day, and he has worn it ever since.

I remember taking off my clothes and jewelry and putting them in a bag. I had to give it all up. It was just me, my hospital gown, and God going into surgery together. The thought ran through my mind, *you can't take it with you.* Putting my watch in the bag, I thought of how prisoners must feel when they have to give everything up.

A nurse came into the room with a number of consent forms and a living will form. I had to sign something that had to do with my living or dying. I also filled out a form that stated that the tissue could be used in a research study. I now realize that any bit of data will help get the researchers closer to a cure.

Just then, the pastor from our church, Buddy Gray, came into the room. He asked if he could pray with us. I was so grateful he came. It was a welcome surprise. He talked about how the Lord works in wonderful ways. Later that morning, he ran into another church member in the parking lot. That man's wife was also having a mastectomy that day, but they hadn't told anyone. Buddy was able to pray with her, too, before her surgery. He later told me, "If you hadn't been here, I wouldn't have been there for them." I thought, *Well there's something good that's come out of this already.* We prayed, and I felt a sense of peace.

Something else wonderful happened before dawn on the day of my surgery. This type-A personality, who had to be in control and make the house, the kids, the husband, the career, and even the dog run smoothly, had to let go.

I realized I was not really in control of anything. God was in control. What a freeing feeling! God was in control of everything in my life. On this morning of major surgery, I put all the worry and fear on Him, and I allowed the Lord to take away my fear. I felt as if He'd wrapped His arms around me.

SIMON THE LION

The Lord had been starting to encourage others through my experiences. After giving a speech at a local church, I was surprised that so many came up to me to tell me what they had been burdened with. It was like we were all talking about the pain and letting it go. I was so honored that so many trusted me enough to share with me the intimate details of their lives. But God tells us to trust Him and let go of worries. Try saying, "Father, take this thing that I cannot handle. I know You can handle it."

It's almost like exercise. When you first start to run, it feels awkward and uncomfortable. But the more you do it, the easier it gets. Exercise your faith by turning over everything to the Lord! He will give you peace and security. No one can separate you from God!

I still worry about some things, and I still practice praying them away. I still feel sick sometimes, too. I also know the feeling when a child is sick. But for many children who end up at Children's of Alabama, being sick is an intense, scary time.

I once interviewed the chaplain at Children's. For someone who cared for almost three hundred patients at any given time at the hospital, he was very calm and peaceful. When I asked him how he ministered to children, he produced a cuddly lion. It was Simon the Lion.

Groups and churches buy the stuffed animals. Then they commit to pray for the children they will probably never meet. It is comforting. The chaplain also showed me some colorful stones they hand out as well. They have the words *peace*, *hope*, and *faith* written on them. Again, a way to offer comfort.

I asked him if he had ever seen miracles at the hospital. He replied, "Yes, almost every day." But he said that sometimes the miracles come with outcomes that we would not choose. The real miracle, he explained, is that in the midst of pain, people can still have hope — they can still find peace during their storms of life.

"Herein lies your security, which not one and no circumstance can take from you."

"For I am the L<small>ORD</small> *your God who takes hold of your right hand and says to you, Do not fear; I will help you"* (Isaiah 41:13).

"Blessed are those who have learned to acclaim you, who walk in the light of your presence, Lord" (Psalm 89:15).

I have felt that presence through cancer, deaths, injuries, and the shocks of life.

"Rejoice always, pray continually" (1 Thessalonians 5:16–17).

What is it that burdens you? Can you truly let it go into God's hands? Soon after I surrender a situation to God, I see progress and His loving hand in it. Is it the people you love that you worry about? Maybe it is a health condition. Perhaps it is a job, business, or a money matter. Do you control things, or do they really control you? Now take a deep breath, and think of the thing that controls you the most. As you exhale, imagine you are releasing this burden. It is floating up to the Lord, and He will handle it for you. Now rest in God's loving power. Bask in the light of His love.

Our Key Scripture

"Surely God is my salvation; I will trust and not be afraid. The Lord, the Lord himself, is my strength and my defense; he has become my salvation" (Isaiah 12:2).

The Glory of Trusting in God

GOD KNOWS WHAT HE'S DOING

On April 27, 2011, my boss tapped me on the shoulder and said, "I need an anchor to go to Cullman. It was just hit by a major tornado. It wrecked the town."

I was to go there and report live how the storm ripped up the downtown area. Driving from Birmingham to Cullman, I had an unusual peace, even though we were driving into the storm and just barely passed the devastating tornado that had hit Tuscaloosa and Pleasant Grove minutes before.

I looked at my smartphone weather radar. I couldn't believe what I was seeing. It looked like tornadoes were marching across the state. Bright pink and red, with the pink forming a C-shape. That perfect C-shape meant that a huge tornado was hitting that area right at that moment. The shape had just passed Pleasant Grove, where my mom, sister, brother-in-law, and nephew lived.

I prayed. I prayed for their safety and for the safety of my children in Hoover. I prayed for my own safety, but I also felt that if the Lord would choose to take me on that day, I was ready. It seemed like a distinct possibility.

I was so thankful that my sister answered my text. They were OK. They said it sounded like a train overhead. When I told her that my supervisors had sent me to Cullman, I got a text back with all caps: *"Why did they send you there!"*

"It's just part of the job," I replied. We warn you it is coming, and we show you the devastation. When we are telling people to get to a safe place, we buckle our own seatbelts and head into the storm. Exciting? Bizarre? Insane? Yes, all of the above. But we, and the emergency crews, head to disaster when it strikes. At that point I still didn't realize that much of my sister's neighborhood had been erased by the tornado. I hadn't yet fathomed the magnitude of what was happening to our state.

I watched as the storms approached the house where my boys were. Again I prayed. I thought that would be it. Throughout the afternoon, the storms seemed to keep coming. I tried to calm my photographer; he had just talked to his wife in Trussville, while she and her baby were crouched in a bathtub! Then the phones went dead. Even though we didn't know for sure about our families' safety, we still had a job to do.

Then the tornado sirens started up in Cullman again! Still, I had peace in the storm. *Lord, if You take me today, I'm ready, but please take care of my loved ones.* How could I have peace in the storm? The Holy Spirit is the only answer.

Part of my job is collecting items to take to storm-hit areas. I giggled when saw spaghetti noodles. The Saturday after the storm, I had planned to go to Pleasant Grove, but the local emergency management agency directed us to McDonald Chapel. It was an incredible scene.

There were boards everywhere. People in shock. People grateful to get what my family and friends delivered. We had food, chicken sandwiches, underwear, socks, deodorant, and soap. Things you would need if you couldn't get out to get anything and had no power. As we were delivering the last few bags, I was almost embarrassed to take the bag with my spaghetti noodles in it. But when I approached the pile of donated items, I saw a basket filled with spaghetti sauce! I put the noodles right next to it and knew God had it all under control.

The people of the storm had a lot of loss and pain to deal with. In our everyday lives, things don't always go the way we want them to. But God can turn those lemons into lemonade if you let Him! After the shock of any storm or struggle can come the pain. That pain can turn into bitterness. You may not be an actual storm victim, but your storm might be a difficult relationship, or it might be job related, or it could be financial. Even raising your children can be a storm.

Yes, being a parent can sometimes feel like you're in a tempest. There are early mornings and late nights. There are homework assignments and sports and other activities to keep up with, not to mention the sudden onset of illness. There are heartbreaks to soothe after lost ball games or lost loves.

For young moms, maybe you are so tired you can't see straight. Your days are filled with mommy duties. You entertain and nurture your baby. You do laundry (a never-ending task, by the way), walk the dog, and make sure a hot meal is on the table.

But you are not along. God sees you where you are. He knows exactly what you are going through. He understands our pain, fatigue, and frustration. He even understands if we are upset with His decisions.

But why should we worry at all? Why should we feel sorry for ourselves?

> "Now listen, you who say, 'Today or tomorrow we will go to this or that city, spend a year there, carry on business and make money.' Why, you do not even know what will happen tomorrow. What is your life? You are a mist that appears for a little while and then vanishes. "Instead, you ought to say, 'If it is the Lord's will, we will live and do this or that.' As it is, you boast in your arrogant schemes. All such boasting is evil" (James 4:13–16).

Keep in mind that arrogance and worry are both sins, and it is never God's will for you to sin. We contribute to life, but we don't control life. God is ultimately in control. He controls the outcome. Let go of worry and the arrogance that allows you to think you have some semblance of control. Instead of worrying, do God's work today.

After that heavy subject, let me lighten things up and tell you about the *Oh Yah Bar*! A man and wife were shopping at the grocery store one day. She heard him gasp and say, "Oh nooooo!" She had two parents with heart problems, so hearing that cry from him made her wonder if he was having a heart attack.

When she turned to look, she was relieved to see that he was just fine. But he was studying the protein bar section very closely. She asked him if he was OK.

"No," he replied. "They don't have my favorite protein bar!"

"Oh, I see!" she answered. She was really relieved it wasn't a 911 situation! She then pointed out that there was another protein bar he could try. "Why don't you try this one? It is the "Oh Yah Bar!"

Begrudgingly, he took the box and agreed to try them. But he muttered, "They probably won't be as good!

A few days later, she was working in the kitchen and heard a shout from the living room. "Oh Yah!" Making sure this wasn't another possible heart attack in progress, she ran to her husband's chair where he was chewing with great pleasure!

He shouted, "This is even better than my old protein bar!" God's plan is always better than ours. I often have a plan, and then God will turn me down a different path. That's when I see that His plan is better! Always. Even if I don't initially like the new plan, I can eventually see His love and wisdom directing me. Have you asked God, *Why me?* It's because He loves you and wants to give you something better.

GAINING A HEAVENLY PERSPECTIVE

God disciplines in love, not hate, and we should too. Here's some new-mom advice. Now that we've sent our oldest son off to college, I look back and want to tell moms, *Worry less, hug and laugh more.* I see young moms so worried about getting every detail right. Remember, there is no test for you at the end of 18 years. Keep them safe, help them the best you can, love them a lot, and let them know they are loved.

Discipline in love; don't punish in spite. Don't exasperate your children, for then they will just stop listening. "Fathers, do not exasperate your children; instead, bring them up in the training and instruction of the Lord" (Ephesians 6:4). A good goal is to be able to look back as a parent and say that you did all you knew how to do. You did your best. In parenting as is in life, love is the greatest of the commandments.

When God deals with us here on earth, He grants some prayers for healing, but not others. But God always works redemptively. He works in different ways for different people. God is sovereign. When we don't understand Him, we need to just trust Him. Trust God's character. We are told in Scripture that we have the mind of God. But why then don't we understand why God does or does not do something when we ask? That's because of our human condition — because we have a selfish nature.

In Isaiah 28, the people of God could not believe that God had allowed bad things to happen to them. Well, God has always been working and continues to work through generations for redemption.

"Now stop your mocking, or your chains will become heavier; the LORD, the LORD Almighty, has told me of the destruction decreed against the whole land. Listen and hear my voice; pay attention and hear what I say. When a farmer plows for planting, does he plow

continually? Does he keep on breaking up and work-
ing the soil? When he has leveled the surface, does he
not sow caraway and scatter cumin? Does he not plant
wheat in its place, barley in its plot, and spelt in its
field? His God instructs him and teaches him the right
way. Caraway is not threshed with a sledge, nor is the
wheel of a cart rolled over cumin; caraway is beaten
out with a rod, and cumin with a stick. Grain must be
ground to make bread; so one does not go on threshing
it forever. The wheels of a threshing cart may be rolled
over it, but one does not use horses to grind grain. All
this also comes from the LORD *Almighty, whose plan*
is wonderful, whose wisdom is magnificent" (22–29).

Sure there are times we can't understand what He is doing. But that's because there is a big picture. God sees the eternal reason; we do not. God allows tough times for our growth and to further the growth of His kingdom.

But we can be encouraged by the fact that when we die, we will live! Because Jesus died for us, we will have everlasting life. It is hard to get our minds around, but consider that each of us is like a seed. In 1 Corinthians 15, Paul compares our flesh to plants:

"How are the dead raised? With what kind of body
will they come? How foolish! What you sow does not
come to life unless it dies. When you sow, you do not
plant the body that will be, but just a seed, perhaps of
wheat or of something else.

"But God gives it a body as he has determined, and to each kind of seed he gives its own body. Not all flesh is the same: People have one kind of flesh, animals have another, birds another and fish another. There are also heavenly bodies and there are earthly bodies; but the splendor of the heavenly bodies is one kind, and the splendor of the earthly bodies is another. The sun has one kind of splendor, the moon another and the stars another; and star differs from star in splendor.

"So will it be with the resurrection of the dead. The body that is sown is perishable, it is raised imperishable; it is sown in dishonor, it is raised in glory; it is sown in weakness, it is raised in power; it is sown a natural body, it is raised a spiritual body" (35–44).

Notice that it is sown in weakness, and then it is raised in power. What a wonderful focus as a Christian. Thanks to the power of God, our weak, frail bodies will be raised in a new form that does not perish. Focusing on the fact that death can have no hold on you should give you confidence beyond belief!

God has a plan. I believe God called many people home during those April 27 storms. And He also found miraculous ways to save people. There were many stories of angels who helped to save people. Some of those stories came in the form of the divine; others came in the form of regular people helping people. An elderly man says an angel told him to get to shelter. His life was spared.

A few years after the big storm in central Alabama, another miraculous story hit the national news. In Quincy, Illinois, there was a terrible accident on the highway. A young lady, 19-year-old Katie Lentz, was trapped in her car. The rescue attempt lasted for hours. Many rescue workers on the scene agreed that it was one of the worst accidents they'd ever seen.

She was pinned inside her car on that hot August day. A rescue worker promised Katie and her mother that he would get her out. But it wasn't going well, and each time he tried to pry her loose, the heavy metal would not budge. Katie's vital signs were starting to fail, and the rescue team said that the chances she would come out of the vehicle alive were grim. At that point, Katie had asked if someone would pray with her and a voice said, "I will."

That voice belonged to a priest who had come walking in from the north. No one can explain how he got through from that direction. The road had been heavily barricaded because of the accident. The priest prayed that the rescue workers would be able to get her out. One of the rescue workers said he heard a voice say, "You will get her out. It will work."

And it did! Shortly after that voice was heard, rescue workers freed the young lady. But the priest disappeared. Even with all the media surrounding the accident scene and everyone taking pictures with their camera phones, not one picture included this mysterious priest.

Because of his unexplained arrival and departure, the national news called this priest an angel. He has now been identified as Father Patrick Dowling, who got to meet Katie a few weeks later.

Whether divine or human in manifestation, I believe miracles happen by God's grace every day. But this one actually made the news. Do you believe God is still in the miracle business? I do!

"He performs wonders that cannot be fathomed, miracles that cannot be counted" (Job 5:9).

"I will remember the deeds of the LORD; yes, I will remember your miracles of long ago" (Psalm 77:11).

"You are the God who performs miracles; you display your power among the peoples" (Psalm 77:14).

The young woman in the accident obviously had faith. She asked for prayer from others, and she prayed to God herself. Do we sometimes get so lax, so comfortable in life and in what we believe, that we are close minded to the possibility of miracles in our lives? Have we lost faith that God can change our circumstance for the better?

When you hear about these miraculous life-saving stories, does it make you ask, *Why were these people saved while others were not?* The answer lies in the hope that we have something beyond this physical world. The Lord has already prepared a place for us. Even though He assured His first disciples of that, He has that assurance available for His followers today and always.

"Do not let your hearts be troubled. You believe in God; believe also in me. My Father's house has many rooms; if that were not so, would I have told you that I am going there to prepare a place for you? And if I go and prepare a place for you, I will come back and

take you to be with me that you also may be where I am. You know the way to the place where I am going.

"Thomas said to him, 'Lord, we don't know where you are going, so how can we know the way?' Jesus answered, 'I am the way and the truth and the life. No one comes to the Father except through me'" (John 14:1–6).

Trust! God has a plan!

In one of those April tornados in 2011, Tom Lee threw himself between the falling debris and his 13 children. As the tornado hit, he died; they lived. What a sacrifice. That is the ultimate act of love. Just as Jesus loved us so much that He died for us.

My dad would say, "I love you kids so much I would die for you!" It is easier to understand the depth of God's love when it's viewed from a parent's perspective. You love them, protect them, and sometimes have to allow them to fall and skin a knee in order for them to grow and get stronger. God loves us so much that He sent His only Son to die for us. Being parents, we can in a tiny way understand how our Father in heaven feels about us.

EVEN CLOSER

After speaking to a group of cancer survivors one Sunday, I ran out of gas and pulled into the nearest gas station. The car in front of me had "BibleUniverse.com" on the rear window. The Mississippi license tag also read "Bible U."

Being a skeptical investigative reporter, I'm ashamed to say that I was a little judgmental. I questioned the authenticity of the Web site and the tag. To make matters worse, the driver then approached me and asked for a dollar. *Now I was sure it was a scam!*

So I prayed quickly, but God moved me to give him some cash anyway. I didn't have a dollar—what I had was more than a dollar. While my hand was in my purse, I wrestled with God. *I am on a budget!* But God kept moving me to hand the bill to him. When he saw it, he said, "All I need is a dollar!" He seemed to want to give me change, but he didn't have any. So he asked, "Can I pray with you?"

That's when I thought, *Uh-oh, this is where I get hit in the head!* But it was the sweetest prayer.

"Lord, thank You for giving us what we need and sometimes giving even more than what we need. Amen."

After praying, he asked me, "Are you sure?"

I said, "Get something to eat. I bet you're hungry!"

I felt so blessed, all the way home! God always provides—even during the storms of life. There were times I felt spoon fed. "He gives strength to the weary and increases the power of the weak" (Isaiah 40:29).

Knowing that He provides for me makes want to be even closer to Him. But even more encouraging is the fact that Jesus prays for me. Did you know that Jesus prays for you?

*"My prayer is not for them alone [the disciples].
I pray also for those who will believe in me through
their message, that all of them may be one, Father,
just as you are in me and I am in you. May they also
be in us so that the world may believe that you have
sent me. I have given them the glory that you gave
me, that they may be one as we are one — I in them
and you in me — so that they be brought to complete unity. Then the world will know that you sent
me and have loved them even as you have loved me.*

*"Father, I want those you have given me to be
with me where I am, and to see my glory, the glory
you have given me because you loved me before
the creation of the world. Righteous Father, though
the world does not know you, I know you, and they
know that you have sent me. I have made you known
to them, and will continue to make you known in
order that the love you have for me may be in them
and that I myself may be in them"* (John 17:20–25).

God loves you! Jesus loves you enough to pray for you, even
long before you were born. Doesn't knowing this about the Lord
encourage you to seek a more intimate relationship with Him?

Our Key Scripture

"Bring joy to your servant, Lord, for I put my trust in you. You, Lord, are forgiving and good, abounding in love to all who call to you. Hear my prayer, Lord; listen to my cry for mercy. When I am in distress, I call to you, because you answer me. Among the gods there is none like you, Lord; no deeds can compare with yours. All the nations you have made will come and worship before you, Lord; they will bring glory to your name. For you are great and do marvelous deeds; you alone are God" (PSALM 86:4–10).

CHAPTER 11

Encouraged

CHIVALRY LIVES ON

During my storms with cancer, the worst parts of the chemo were the pokes in the arm. Husband, Doug, had been my bodyguard through the surgery, recovery, and through the chemotherapy. He drove me to my treatments.

During each treatment, Doug would walk me into the room where the nurse would put the pick line — a tube they would attach the chemo line to — into my arm. The needle and subsequent tube would have to be placed just right. I am not blessed with big veins, so this always presented a challenge for the nurse to find just the right vein to invade.

On one particular treatment day, I felt the worst pain of all during this process. She couldn't find a vein that worked, so she had to "go shopping for one," as she put it. That meant poke, after poke, after poke. I had to get up and go to the bathroom to splash cold water on my face. I felt faint and nauseated by the pain.

While I was in there, my dear, sweet husband who stands about six feet, four inches tall, was talking to my nurse. He said, "You aren't going to hurt Brenda any more, are you?" Even though the bathroom door was closed, I could see him towering over the petite woman.

He wasn't threatening—just trying to strongly encourage her to get it done with the least amount of pain possible. He could be like such a guard dog when it comes to his family. It is an admirable trait. I smiled at the thought that he loved me so much that he would do anything to protect me.

This big strong man—who cringes and turns away if he sees a stranger get a shot in the arm on TV shows or news reports—stood by me during each poke. He winced with me. We weren't just two people in that room; we were as one. I opened the door and smiled at my knight in shining armor.

"You aren't scaring the nurses, are you, honey?" I asked. He gave me his sheepish smile.

Then the nurse smiled and said, "Let's get this over with."

I silently hoped that she wouldn't punish me for bringing in my bodyguard. I said the Lord's Prayer to myself. And it's a miraculous thing . . . she found the right vein! The poking was over! And just to be fair, I have to mention that at my next chemo session, she got the vein on the very first try!

No local woman's chemo battle is complete without a visit to Touching You, a specialty shop for women with cancer. Carol Cauthen, the owner of the shop, is also a breast cancer survivor. She shared her own experience with me. In fact, I vaguely remembered that she had come to visit me in the hospital, while I was under morphine shortly after surgery.

Her story inspired me. She told me how she continued to go to work, even during her chemo. She counseled me about the hair loss. She even cried with me. She said this business was her way of giving back. I felt very safe while in her company. If she could survive and go on to have a son, against all the odds that her doctors had given her, then I could beat this thing too!

Doug even accompanied me on my Touching You ventures. I remember making one visit there after my surgery to buy some specially-designed supportive undergarments for mastectomy patients who have been reconstructed. I had to be measured, because I wasn't really sure what size Dr. Beckenstein had provided me with. Not every man would be brave enough to walk through those doors. I knew Doug was going through so much inside as well.

Whenever my husband was near me during the recovery from surgery or the chemotherapy, I felt better. I felt complete. His support and encouragement have meant so much.

THE CHEMO COMMUNITY

What could possibly be good about sitting around for a couple of hours getting chemo or poison pumped into your arm? Making friends with people who are traveling the same path you are on. These are people dealing with the same scary statistics, uncertainties, and pain. They really understand.

On one of those visits for chemo, I met a sweet lady with whom I instantly felt a bond. Her name is Francis Farmer. We started talking about what helped beat the side effects from chemo. We were excited to find out that walking had a similar effect for both of us. It helped our energy levels, and also helped fend off the nausea. Francis still calls to check on me, and I embrace her calls. I'm inspired to know she's doing OK, and that her cancer has stayed away. She breathes a sigh of relief for me too. I say, "Please stay in touch." And I know she will.

We really do have a team. We survivors help root each other on. Walking into the cancer center can be like a team meeting—a pep rally, if you will. These are many of the same people you see week after week or month after month.

I am so encouraged by the story of a woman with advanced-stage breast cancer. She had been given only a matter of months to live. But she proudly told me, with a twinkle in her eye (almost like a child who got away with something), that it had been four years now and the cancer was under control. The treatments were working! There is such hope there in the waiting room.

When I looked around that hospital room, I didn't see sick people. I saw survivors! Warriors! People who were giving it their all to beat a killer. People in the waiting room would chat like long lost friends. One particular day, the daughter of that same inspiring advanced-stage woman walked over to an elderly man. She chatted with him and then went to retrieve a cup of cold water for him.

At first I thought they were related. But after hearing them talk, I realized that this was just another friendship made at the Cancer Center. I remember thinking, *Too bad we couldn't all meet under more pleasant circumstances.* But no, we wouldn't have nearly the bond we have now.

That's something cancer can do. It can bring people together, or drive them apart. That can be an individual's choice. But reaching out and allowing someone to help you get through it is one way to cope and live through what seems impossible.

FAMILY TIES

A few days after I returned home and was resting in bed, the phone rang. It was my surgeon, Dr. Susan Winchester. I was very impressed that a busy surgeon would take the time to call.

"How are you?" she asked.

"Oh, I'm fine, thanks," I responded as if it were any other day.

"No, how are you *really* doing? How's the depression?" she asked.

"The depression?" I asked.

She went on to explain that many women experience depression as part of the aftersurgery healing process.

I said, "No, I'm not really depressed, but I'll work on it."

After we hung up, I thought about it. I realized that there had been those moments. One time when I had been on powerful pain medicine, I remember thinking, *What would people think of me now? Would my husband still love me? Could I go on? Would I ever be "Mommy" again?*

Was it depressing dealing will the aftereffects of surgery? Was it depressing knowing I'd have to undergo chemotherapy and lose my hair because cancer had invaded two lymph nodes? Yes. Did I cry? You betcha! In fact, I can still hear Dr. Susan's voice: "Crying is great for healing and for the immune system." It was a regular part of my healing process. So go ahead and cry. It's OK.

Even during those down times, I still felt like a child holding onto the Lord's hand. He led me through, every step of the way. I kept one of my favorite verses running through my mind: "Trust in the LORD with all your heart; do not depend on your own understanding" (Proverbs 3:5 NLT). Have you memorized it yet?

Yes, cancer has been a life-changing experience. Just imagine your former job rivals and competitors becoming like sisters and brothers instantly. Two particular people whom I had competed with over the years come to mind. I had even prayed for them occasionally, because I thought they would just as soon have thrown me in a lake rather than look at me. Surprisingly, they came to me and embraced me with their love and support during my storm. God is good.

But most important of all, my journey mended a rift in my own family, one that I had been praying about for months before I was diagnosed—it reunited my two sisters. Linda and Susan have an oil-and-water kind of relationship. The divide between them had occurred months earlier, and they had hardly spoken since. But while Linda was in town helping to care for me, she and Susan were forced to talk on the phone.

I had just made one of my valiant attempts to traverse a few feet from my bed to the bathroom all on my own. While sitting there, I saw bugs climbing the walls, but I knew it was just the morphine. I thought I saw smoke wisping up the walls as well. Oh well, at least the morphine was doing its job for the pain, for the most part.

While I was still pondering the smoke and bugs, I heard the phone ring. I could hear Linda: "Hello? Uh, she's in the bathroom right now. Oh, well this is Linda . . . . OK, I'll tell her you called." And that was it . . . the bottle of oil and water had been shaken up during this storm, even if just a little bit. They had at least talked, and that was good. I was the catalyst for their healing to begin.

Before cancer (in my BC days), these were things that I was always too busy for. But now I had time, and plenty of it. Linda also helped me go through the hundreds of cards and letters that poured in. We were both overwhelmed by the love and support from so many people. I told her I lived in a great community where the people were so caring. Card after card read, *We're praying for you. Get well soon.* I could hear God speaking right through them. They were encouraging and uplifting. With all those prayers, I knew I'd have to get up out of this bed and be Brenda again.

RECEIVING *A* ROCK FROM *THE* ROCK

How would you react if you asked for a blessing and God delivered a bag of rocks to you instead? *Sometimes our blessing and answers to prayer are not obvious.* When that happens, we still have to keep the faith.

I prayed for God to show me my mission in life, and one month later I found a lump. Then I got my diagnosis. I am a fixer . . . so how do you fix cancer? *There's a killer in the neighborhood. I have to warn others!* I could sense that this was going to be a big part of my mission: to warn people about cancer, to urge early detection.

But through it all, I have found a mission field comprised of more than just people who have cancer. I'm also here to encourage *all* people not to fear *anything* in this world. We all need encouragement, and that's why we all are here. Grab hold of God, and let go of fear.

Through cancer, God has revealed so many hidden blessings. Like a more intimate prayer life. I have come to totally put myself in His arms. I can really feel His presence daily.

God had a plan for my life, and it was good. He has healed me. My God always answers prayers. It may not always be the exact answer we are looking for. But we are at the top of His "To Do" list!

As part of my mission to encourage, I was asked to speak to Lynne Baptist Church, which was more than an hour drive away. That morning, my 14-year-old son Garrett hopped in the car with me, and we headed northwest. It was one of those perfectly gorgeous October days. The sky was crystal clear blue, with not a bit of humidity. The drive was beautiful, with the trees starting to change from green to yellow, and orange to red. We enjoyed a variety of music, from religious-inspirational to country, on the car CD player.

When we arrived in the tiny town of Lynne, Alabama, we noticed it was completely surrounded by farmland. On this Sunday morning there were few people outside, except for a man and his son doing yard work in front of their house. I figured that most people were already in church, and my guess was proved right. When we arrived, Sunday school was already underway. I had just enough time to run a brush through my hair before the service began.

I sat with my son as the service started. It was a beautiful old church with a high ceiling held up with heavy wooden beams. As the music minister reached the pulpit, I wondered what song he had picked. Then, as the words flashed on the overhead screen and the first notes were belted out, tears welled up in my eyes. I whispered to Garrett, "I think I'm gonna cry! That was Pap Pap's favorite song!" Whenever I hear it, I can still picture him sitting at the old family piano which is more than 200 years old now. He would belt out "How Great Thou Art" like there was no tomorrow. He would hold nothing back.

Yes, it was a sweet memory and a reminder of how the love of God was passed down through the family. I got up to speak and apologized for crying my makeup off after hearing the song that was so near and dear to my father's heart. I spoke that day about how we are called to encourage one another and love one another. I talked about holding on to the Lord through the storms of life. The Lord also reminded me to remind the people of the church that they are blessed, that they should focus on what they have, not what they don't have. Their loving response was a blessing to me that day, and it did not matter that I was crying. I did not have to be Superwoman, just His daughter.

Our Key Scripture

"Praise be to the God and Father of our Lord Jesus Christ, the Father of compassion and the God of all comfort, who comforts us in all our troubles, so that we can comfort those in any trouble with the comfort we ourselves receive from God" (2 CORINTHIANS 1:3–4).

CHAPTER 12

Called to Encourage

LITTLE GIVER

The happiest people are givers. They focus on the needs of others, giving of themselves. In focusing on God first, life is put into perspective. He will help you with your burdens, and then you can use the power you find in Christ to minister to those around you.

This letter came to me from a father who is extremely proud of his daughter.

> "My daughter Emily will be turning 16 on September 8 of this year. Like most Moms and Dads, we wanted to make sure that her Sweet 16th birthday party would be all she imagined. Several weeks ago we began to discuss with Emily what she wanted for her birthday and where she wanted to have her party. As we sat with pen in hand and paper in front of me ready to write down an enormous list of requests, she began to lay out her birthday plan to her mother and me.

"'Dad,' she said, 'There is a little boy in our church who is two years old who has a very severe medical condition. You see, Dad, he has seizures, and his medicine costs his parents several thousands of dollars a month out of their pockets. Insurance doesn't cover the entire cost.' As she continued talking, I obviously was intrigued by her story. She went on to tell me that the parents were unable to keep their home, and every waking minute and every extra penny they have goes toward medical expenses.

"She simply said that she wanted nothing for her birthday—not one present or gift. She has asked that her sweet 16th birthday party become a fundraiser for the sweet little boy known as Baby Tripp. As a daddy, I began to weep, realizing that success as a father was sitting across the table from me.

"With that being said, her mother and I are renting several large inflatables, and she is inviting many people from the Chelsea community, along with Baby Tripp and his family, to come and enjoy the DJ. Everyone will have a great time and at the same time raise money for a sweet family.

"I am a captain for the City of Pelham Fire Department, and I have seen my fair share of bad things in life. However, after hearing my sweet baby girl tell me she wanted to forgo what should be her biggest birthday, and give it all to a little boy and his family,

I know there is still good in people, and I am so proud
to call Emily my little girl."

CLOSE CALL

Not many people experience losing all their possessions and nearly
losing their lives. But I imagine it feels like having a rug pulled
out from under you. I remember getting the call from my friend
Gena just after they'd lost everything in a fire. Here's how the
story goes.

At 3:00 on the morning of the fire, 11-month-old Anna
couldn't sleep. So, like any good toddler, she entertained herself
by rummaging through a box full of some old videotapes. The
noise woke up her mother Gena. Anna had grabbed a hold of the
tape of Gena's wedding, so Gena decided to pop it in the VCR to
lull them both back to sleep.

It was a beautiful service. It even solidified her marriage in her
mind . . . watching them at the altar again. Gena believes the Lord
allowed her to see it and emblazon it into her memory just hours
before her house burned completely to the ground.

Gena's boys were two and four. That night the boys asked if
they could sleep in their big sister Katherine's room. She was six at
the time. Gena at first said no, that they needed to sleep in their own
twin beds. But it was unusual that they insisted, so she relented. No
one knew it at the time, but, just on the other side of the wall next
to her sons' beds, their water heater had sprung a gas leak.

Gena's husband Bill had to leave for work at 6:45. He was letting the family sleep in because it was summer and they had got-

ten in late from a trip. Then the phone rang. Bill picked it up and continued talking to his dad for about ten minutes. This was a gift from the Lord, because his father rarely called at this time of day.

After Bill hung up, he jumped in his car. But he remembered that he'd forgotten to brush his teeth, so again he went back inside. Another gift from God?

That's when he heard the fire alarm going off. Gena was still asleep and didn't wake up to the alarm. They now know that the natural gas leak had put her into a deep sleep. As Bill was waking Gena, he could see smoke rolling down the hallway. The den was also on fire. It seemed to take an eternity to wake Gena up, and then they both ran to get the children out.

Running through the thick black smoke, they could feel the heat from the fire. They could barely breathe as they raced for the front door. But the front door handle was so hot that Bill couldn't grab it. Gena took off one of the boys' shirts for Bill to use, but by then the doorframe had swelled, and he couldn't pull the door open. So Bill went to get a chair.

About that time, four-year-old William said, "Dear Lord, please let our door open." Even though Gena had little Anna on her hip, after she heard that prayer, she decided to give the door one more tug, and it opened. Just as they finally got out of the house, the water heater exploded, tearing up the two boys' bedroom and blowing out every window in the house. Gina said that it sounded like someone had taken a baseball bat and broken out each window one by one down the line.

They ran across the street to a neighbor's house. They were all in shock. The children could see their stuffed animals were burning. The fireman said to Bill, "If you had not been there, I would have been calling you to come identify your family."

The house was a total loss. Gena and Katherine went back inside after the fire was put out. The remains of the house were still, and the only thing they could identify in the melted and deformed kitchen was the stench. It seemed to represent evil and darkness. Even little Katherine picked up on this, and she asked if this is what hell looked like.

Gena replied, "No, this is just a picture. Hell is so much worse, because you are separated from God and there's no light."

The fire had taken all their belongings. Everything from clothes to books. But Gena tells me that the most disturbing things they lost were pictures: family pictures, wedding pictures, baby pictures, videos of the children taking their first steps, and the wedding video she had looked at just hours before. They could not be replaced. Gena lost her grandmother's ring, and a quilt that had been handed down for generations. Her grandmother had passed away just months before the fire. From her Greek side of the family, she lost the silver that had also been passed down.

The little kids needed clothes, and so did Mom and Dad. We went digging into our closets to find some things to share. But we weren't alone. God's goodness from the family of Christ started pouring in. Clothes, stuffed animals, and more. People sent food and gift cards to help. People throughout the whole community pitched in to do anything they could. The Lord was providing. Of course, Gena says that the best gift that God gave her was to spare her children.

I told you that story so I can tell this one. Flip the pages of time forward, up to that terrible April 27 day when all those tornadoes ripped through the state. Thousands of people lost just about everything. Guess who called me offering to help. It was Gena. She jumped right in to organize a group of high school students to help pick up the pieces in Pleasant Grove. She and the teens were working to help a man sift through the rubble after the tornado had leveled his house. Gina saw one of the teens pick up half of a picture that was tattered and torn. Before he could throw it away, she grabbed it and gave it to the man. It was part of a wedding photo. She knew how precious that picture was to him.

They also found a family Bible, and he teared up when they found some old pictures their children had drawn. She told him, "I know what it's like to lose everything." He smiled but he couldn't get any words to come out. She said, "I know," and she really did.

She later told me, "I know what it's like to lose everything, but it's losing the family pictures that really hurts. I know how they feel, and I know I can comfort them, because I've been there."

"Let us draw near to God with a sincere heart and with the full assurance that faith brings, having our hearts sprinkled to cleanse us from a guilty conscience and having our bodies washed with pure water. Let us hold unswervingly to the hope we profess, for he who promised is faithful. And let us consider how we may spur one another on toward love and good deeds, not giving up meeting together, as some are in the habit of doing, but encouraging

one another — and all the more as you see the Day
approaching" (Hebrews 10:22–25).

The fire changed Gena and her family forever. It made them more empathetic. They now have a heart to encourage others in need.

HER LEFT FOOT

Nequia Underwood gives us another example of being able to get through anything. When I met her, she was 19 years old. Her mother Janice wanted to share her story with me, because she wanted to help encourage others.

Nequia was born with a foot deformity. Her mother explained that she looked like a ballerina all the time. Her feet did not bend at the ankle at all. Her mother prayed for God to help her daughter. Her husband was just finishing up his time in the military, and they would soon lose their medical insurance. One day after praying for an answer for her little girl, Janice was walking in the mall with Nequia in the stroller, and she saw a man asking for donations.

"Therefore if you have any encouragement from
being united with Christ, if any comfort from his love,
if any common sharing in the Spirit, if any tender-
ness and compassion, then make my joy complete
by being like-minded, having the same love, being
one in spirit and of one mind. Do nothing out of
selfish ambition or vain conceit. Rather, in humility
value others above yourselves, not looking to your

own interests but each of you to the interests of the others" (Philippians 2:1–4).

Janice has a big heart, and although she herself was in a financial bind, she reached into her purse and pulled out a dollar to give the man. He gave her a pamphlet in return. She read it as she walked away, then stopped dead in her tracks and made an about-face to go back to talk to this older man with a weathered, kind face.

The pamphlet told about an organization that helps children like Nequia! She asked him if this was true, and he said yes. He also gave her other helpful information about the hospital and the doctors.

It turns out that her act of kindness was rewarded a thousand times. The Shriners paid for many years of surgeries to help correct Nequia's feet. Today she can walk. She even models, and has big plans for her future.

God blessed Janice with a pure, giving heart. In truth, she had needed every dollar she had. But through her generosity and love for others, she gave anyway. She just trusted the Lord, not intending to be rewarded. But the Holy Spirit moved her to help a brother. That is how God's love works. That is how God encourages. That is how God restores. While you are in a storm. . . .

THIS NEWS JUST ARRIVED

One final story for now. . . . Wow, this blew me away as I finished my final chapter for you. I received an amazing email as this book and the *Encouraged* DVD were getting finishing touches for release in stores and online:

> Brenda,
>
> Thank you for your reply. I would be glad to have you share my story as that is my goal that I will help someone through what I learn during this journey I now refer to as my *reset*. I am glad I could encourage you! That is just confirmation I am getting God's message that I am to learn and do something with what I learn through this.
>
> I wanted to thank you for the book and shirt you gave me at the . . . conference last week. I am the nurse that spoke to you and told you I am about to start chemotherapy this week for colon cancer. I cannot put your book down and the soft T-shirt comforts me on my walks and reminds me to "Trust in God."
>
> *When I found out I had cancer a few weeks ago I kept seeing my funeral.*
>
> Every time I closed my eyes, I kept seeing my friends and family staring at a table with flowers, pictures, and all of my accomplishments and awards from my 20 years as a nurse. It bothered me so much.

I just wanted to get rid of all of that [imagery]. I was having a hard time staying positive.

After I spoke to you and you hugged me, those funeral visions went away and this big red Reset button appeared in my thoughts. I felt strength in God like I have never felt before. I felt a strong message from God, telling me this is an *opportunity* He is giving me: to Reset. I feel he is [impressing on] me to take some time and learn through this journey and do something with it.

The vision of my funeral and that table has not come back again. I do keep seeing the Reset button but it's a good thing and a reminder that I need to use my time off work to reset, prioritize, and find a way to help others with what I learn through this. I start chemotherapy on Wednesday this week and I feel ready.

Thank you again for speaking at our conference and for taking time to talk to me. I wanted to talk with you longer but forced myself to walk away as I wanted the other attendees to have the opportunity to speak to you as well.

I feel like you saved my life last Thursday and I will never forget it! I hope one day I can help someone as much as you have helped me.

Thanks again Brenda!

God Bless!

Chris

Let me simply give this postscript: Being in a storm means being readied to be encouraged by God, because He has a plan for you to do as He commands — to comfort others who are in any trouble with the comfort you will receive from God (see 2 Corinthians 1:3–5). As others in this book are, as you can be, and as you can share: be encouraged in Jesus' name!

Brenda

Use the QR reader on your
smartphone to visit us online at
NewHopeDigital.com

If you've been blessed by this book, we would like to hear your story.
The publisher and author welcome your comments and
suggestions at: newhopereader@wmu.org.

Get
Encouraged

Visit NewHopeDigital.com/women